The
Supermum
Myth

The Supermum Myth

Overcome anxiety, ditch guilt,
embrace imperfection

**Anya Hayes with
Dr Rachel Andrew**

white
LADDER

This first edition published in Great Britain in 2017 by White Ladder, an imprint of Crimson Publishing Ltd, 19–21c Charles Street Bath BA1 1HX.

British Library Cataloguing in Publication Data

A catalogue record for this book is available from the British Library.

ISBN 978 19103 363 42

Typeset by IDSUK (DataConnections) Ltd

Printed and bound in the United States of America

Contents

About the authors

Anya Hayes is a pregnancy, parenting and wellness writer, and a Pilates teacher specialising in pregnancy and postnatal classes. She is the author of three other books: *My Pilates Guru, A Little Course in Pilates* and *Pregnancy: The Naked Truth*. Anya lives in South East London with her husband and two young sons, and is a lover of yoga, bright lipstick and a glass of red.

Anya blogs at motherswellnesstoolkit.wordpress.com. Come and hang out with her on Instagram: @mothers.wellness.toolkit, or on Twitter: @anyapilates.

Dr Rachel Andrew is a clinical psychologist who has been working with children and families for over 14 years. Dr Rachel began her career working in the NHS, before setting up her company Time Psychology Ltd. She is passionate about sharing psychological knowledge and finding innovative ways to do this. She often works with journalists and television companies. She was first seen on screen in Channel 4's BAFTA nominated *Don't Make Me Angry*. She has also appeared in the BBC's *Fix My Family* series, ITV's *Tonight* programme and BBC Four's *The Cinema Show*. Her expertise can be found in publications ranging from *The Debrief* and *The Pool* to the *Telegraph, Prima, SAGA* and the *Guardian*.

Dr Rachel is married and mum to two young girls. Although tempted to constantly strive for perfection, she can also occasionally find her 'good enough' whilst swimming, with family or immersed in a good drama. Find her on twitter @timepsychology and at www.timepsychology.com.

Acknowledgements

From Anya:

Thank you to everyone who has helped to bring this book to life. It's like birthing a baby – it takes huge effort and energy (and a lot of chocolate biscuits) to create a book. Hopefully, in bringing this book to being you've helped me to help loads of mums build a more positive and happy mum life.

To Dr Rachel Andrew for providing a brilliant and constant stream of psychological resources, activities, imaginings, and for dealing with my requests and suggestions with such calm poise at all times. Between the two of us throughout the course of writing this book we have negotiated chicken pox, myriad other childhood ailments/disasters, half terms and school holidays and we've still managed to get some coherent words on the page. High fives to us.

To Beth Bishop for bringing the project to fruition. Thank you!

To all the women who agreed to be interviewed for the book and who were so open and honest and offered me such a vast array of thoughts, experiences, anecdotes. Quite simply this book wouldn't have materialised without you. Thank you especially to Kelly Abel, Suze Hemming, Emma Burbidge, Hannah Horne, Amy Steadman, Elizabeth Cohen, Antonia Godber, Cee Olaleye, Vicki Moore, Zoe Donkin, Hannah de Lasti, @asideorderofme: you are all true supermums.

To all my Pilates clients and Mothers' Wellness mamas, you have been a wealth of learning and camaraderie for me on my own motherhood journey. Thanks for sharing with me your experiences and thoughts honestly. I really feel honoured to do the work that I do and to be able to work with mums to fine-tune their body and spirit and simply help them feel better as they shepherd their children day to day.

And finally, to my family: to my mum, for being so endlessly loving and patient with my teenage self (even today). To my two wonderful bonkers boys Maurice and Freddie – thank you for truly making me understand the value of Time, by challenging my ownership of this intangible commodity with guaranteed illness or A&E trips when a chapter was due to be finished. I love you more than words can ever express. And to Ben, for being amazing, for cooking meals, for doing bedtime every night so that I can teach and write, for being there. Thank you for knowing I needed to follow my heart and write this book, and for giving me the space to do it.

From Rachel:

A massive thank you to Anya. You have shown such grit and determination in bringing this book about. Thanks for showing me how really great books are written. Thanks to Beth too – I've always dreamt of writing a book – thank you for giving me the opportunity.

Thank you to all the mums I know. This book is for you. To let you know that it is OK to be good enough. It is OK to take a moment, to take care of yourself, and to acknowledge your vulnerabilities.

Thank you to all the women who have had the courage to sit in my room and tell me their stories. It has been a privilege to share your journeys. Thank you to the women I know who have survived bereavements, loss, trauma, separation and illness. Your determination (in the face of overwhelming sadness, hopelessness, anxiety, guilt and anger) has inspired this book.

Thank you to the many people I have met who have taught me that 'mums' come in all shapes and sizes – as grandmas, dads, step-parents, foster carers, teachers. Sometimes children attach themselves to other really important people in their lives. In this book, therefore, the term 'mum' can refer to any person serving as a maternal figure.

Thank you to my children – Madeleine and Emmeline – my strong, powerful girls. Thanks for challenging all I thought I knew – life is richer because of you. To my husband Dominic for quietly encouraging, supporting and holding us all together. And to Joanne, you are a really good friend.

Thank you to my mum and grandmas – the original supermums that I watched and learnt from. You can stop saving the world now, mum. Take a rest. Read the book.

Introduction

Being a mum is both magical and boringly ordinary, and an incredibly vulnerable state of being. As the quote from Elizabeth Stone goes, '... to have a child ... is to decide forever to have your heart walking around outside your body'. Your heart, your decisions, your choices – all suddenly in the open, for judgement and critique. And that judgement and critique can really hit hard. When you're sleep deprived and running on empty, some days it feels like every other mum is doing a much 'better' job than you.

The dictionary definition of a supermum is: 'An exemplary or exceptional mother, especially one who successfully manages a home and brings up children while also having a full-time job.' In our society there is relentless pressure for women to be exceptional at *everything*: gold-star mother, excellent partner, dedicated career woman, committed friend – there are multiple challenges that mums have to face every day, and becoming a multi-tasking queen can feel like a prerequisite. Of course, Supermum has this nailed. The rest of us struggle with this very precarious balancing act.

In reality, even those we crown supermums *are* struggling. You never know what's going on behind someone's glossy façade. Supermum simply does not exist. Deep inside her perfectly fashionable ankle boot, unobservable to the naked eye, her sock is probably sliding off. As a society, we're not open and honest enough about how hard it is to be a mum – as a result you feel acutely aware that the wheels are falling off your wagon and all you can see are mums speeding effortlessly past you. They are not.

The Supermum Myth is about learning to recognise your strengths, and embrace the fact that you *can't* be perfect at everything. The goal is to find out how to be 'you' as a parent, to trust your instincts, and stop comparing yourself to anyone else. Once you learn to notice your self-limiting thoughts, behaviours and actions, you see that your sense of underachievement is purely down to self-belief ... or lack of. This book will help you focus on overturning these unhelpful thoughts and behaviours, offering a toolkit of activities you can dip into every day that will truly revolutionise the happiness levels of your daily mum life.

Perceptions of motherhood

Motherhood is the one thing able to send you from feeling like a million dollars to a piece of poo, in one swoosh of a baby wipe. It contains our zenith, and our nadir. You're having a great mothering day: you wake up after three hours' unbroken sleep (which constitutes a great night), you manage to have a shower, feed and clothe your children, brush all teeth and bundle everyone out the door vaguely on time. You're feeling bloody amazing. Then BAM! A thoughtless comment from someone slaps you round the face, making you feel like crap:

'You had an emergency caesarean? That must be because you had an epidural. I managed on just lavender oil for all my home births.'

'I've lost too much weight since having Alfie because I've been running 10k every day since he was two months old. My clothes are *falling off* – it's so embarrassing!'

'My two have always slept like a dream. I think it's probably because I'm quite a chilled-out mum – they can sense that. Maybe if you were more relaxed your children would sleep better?'

'You don't do *any* after-school activities? Lily goes to taekwondo, ballet, pottery and Mandarin – she's the only four-year-old in the class but the teacher says she's never met such an advanced pupil!'

We've all met that perfect supermum: at the school bake sale, her array of home-made organic gluten-free delights displayed proudly while your last-minute supermarket-bought muffins skulk in the background. She's on the PTA and helps to arrange the school disco, her children eat a variety of food (organic, prepared from scratch). She doesn't know what 'Peppa Pig babysitting' even means. She always has wipes in her bag and an endless supply of snacks and patience ... and there you are, just about getting through the parenting tunnel in a perpetual fog of dry shampoo and coffee, frantically bribing your toddler to potty train with chocolate fingers for breakfast.

Looking a little deeper, you may be able to recognise that, depending on the day, time, moment, that perfect supermum *is* you, *sometimes*.

Imagine those moments when you're not judging yourself harshly, because all is calm – when you are the fleetingly glossy school-gates mum kissing your smiling child goodbye, running happily after the non-tantruming toddler, no glitches, no hitches, no spanners – how would you look to another mum in the playground in those moments? It's all about your own perception.

When you become a mum you become hyper absorbent, soaking up everything, sensitive to everything that is sent your way via judgement, or the way people react to you, or to your children. And, at the same time, we all turn a bit judgy-pants too – and that's not really surprising as being a mum necessarily brings out incredibly strong opinions and emotions, for perhaps the first time in your life. When you judge that mum for looking at her phone at the moment her two-year-old falls off a climbing frame, or for reacting angrily to a tantrum rather than exhibiting endless serenity and patience, place yourself in her moment – wonder what her morning has been like, what she might actually be checking on her phone, what buttons have been pushed preceding that moment, and second-guess your immediate reaction.

A 2016 study of 2,000 mums in the UK (a chocolate-filled crêpe company commissioned the survey, possibly acknowledging that being a mum and eating chocolate is a marriage made in heaven) revealed more than half have a number of friends and acquaintances who 'portray themselves as the perfect mother'. But 60% claim they find these kinds of mums 'highly irritating', while nearly three-quarters dislike it when mums 'show off their prowess on social media'. So it's a tricky internal tug of war – we are collectively reaching for an unattainable ideal of supermum perfection, but we also sort of hate those smug mums who appear to have achieved it.

This is a book for those seeking to find a shift in perception and stop the tugging from one side to the other. Through learning about the psychology behind our core belief system, and breaking down *why* we react and behave the way that we do, we can work out how we have come to our supermum imagined ideal. Then we can learn how to turn it around: to change your reactions to perceived judgements, view your own achievements in a different light, be kinder to yourself – and, by implication, to others. We're all struggling with our own battles.

This book will help you to rebuild your confidence in your own intrinsic wisdom, and drown out the niggling competitive doubts that can grow to cause some serious psychological problems: low self-esteem, anxiety and depression. The sooner you do this, the sooner you can get on with the business of being the brilliant parent you are. Embracing the imperfect, and being good enough. It's not about lowering your expectations of yourself, it's about accepting and acknowledging how well you're doing.

The background to your supermum ideal

Your vision of perfect motherhood is formulated before your baby is even out of the womb – possibly before having even taken up residence in there. We have all sorts of imagined pictures of motherhood in our minds, created through life experiences, from parenting ideals to disasters from our own mums' parenting. The vision of an ideal mum is drip-fed to us through advertising, in the perfect smiles and immaculate hair, in the stereotypical 'one of each' family, in *Topsy and Tim*'s robotic mother who is always the unrattled picture of patience and virtue. And we silently want to kill her.

A 'good' mother is always calm, patient, kind. Her children never kick off wildly because they inexplicably don't want to drink from that blue cup. Remember the time pre-kids when you were shopping and witnessed a bedraggled mother lose her rag with her toddler in Sainsbury's? Maybe you tutted smugly, thinking, 'I will *never* be that kind of mother. I will always be zen. My children will definitely never be feral beasts. I feel sad for that poor child because his mum is so undignified, so unloving, no wonder he's out of control'. Remember those days when you were the best smug parent you could ever be because you didn't have children of your own to test your theory of your future supermum perfection?

Your concept of who you are as a person is formed through your natural temperament, your early childhood (including how you were parented), and all your subsequent life experiences that have created your life story. Your beliefs about yourself and the world are shaped through this – how you relate to others and your emotions are a result of this belief system.

And before you pop a baby out, chances are you imagine that you'll carry on feeling, thinking, working and maintaining relationships exactly as you did before you had children – how hard can it be, right? You may have had images of patiently attending to all your child's physical, emotional and craft-based needs, a Mona Lisa smile on your face at all times, and absolutely no bribing with biscuits or putting on the TV just so you can go to the loo without company.

So it can come as a bit of a shock when the reality is that simply getting out the door in the morning can become a struggle of *Krypton Factor* proportions, and that if you get to work without too much yoghurt in your hair this counts as a sartorial triumph.

I remember when pregnant with my first, going round to a friend's house for dinner. She has three kids, and was cooking dinner for me and some other friends who were also parents. We didn't eat before 9p.m. due to bedtime mayhem. I was inwardly irritated by this, thinking it was down to her not being organised. Conversation echoed with knowing laughter around family domestic arrangements: how having a shower once a week can sometimes feel like a triumph in the early days, and you want to punch your partner who has a shower before cycling to work, then probably another shower at work, and then smugly parades their ultra showering ability in your face on a hot summer's day by coming home from work and, before taking the baby from you, says they need another shower as they're sweaty.

I laughed along, thinking, wow ... not making time to have a shower every day, I mean, that's just crazy talk – what are these women *doing* with their time? Yes, I soon learnt the error of my smug ways. But I think we all have probably felt similar, that we were never going to be *that* mum, to make *those* mistakes. We'll be organised, calm, patient and firm. So to find out that actually you're a scatty, biscuit-bribing, shouty pushover can come as a real shock to the system.

Motherhood can present a battle between our pre-baby self and our mum self, the constant internal 'I never thought I'd be the kind of mum who ...'. I never thought I'd be the kind of mum who bargains with her child about getting dressed or brushing teeth – never bargain with your child, thought the pre-child me, why would you negotiate with a child rather than be in control as the parent? Hmm. And I never used to be the kind of person who would dream of leaving the house with her pants on proud display through an unzipped-up skirt. Now, I am, apparently.

This is good-enough motherhood. Occasionally in a dishevelled state of unshowered pants-in-full-view disarray. Topsy and Tim's mum no doubt never left the house unwashed, and certainly never unaware of being in a state of slight undress. Well, frankly, screw you, Topsy and Tim's mum, you are a figment of a children's TV producer's imagination.

The internet is awash with mum blogs, hashtags and handles with the recurrent theme of Being a Bad Mum: 'bad mum', 'terrible mother', 'guilty mother', 'the guilty mothers' club', '#badparent', '#mumfail', 'parenting fail', 'notparentingtheshitoutoflife'. This is a reflection of our ongoing struggle as mums with not living up to our own, and society's, expectations of what we should be as mothers. Pre-empting others' judgement by judging ourselves as failing.

The Supermum Myth aims to help you lift yourself up on those days you feel you're failing at motherhood, when all you seem to see is images of Instagram feeds full of smiling mums cherishing perfect '#blessed' mothering moments, when you feel your life in comparison is a shambolic mountain of Weetabix-encrusted Lego.

Negative feelings such as envy creep in, and we judge other (super) mums as 'smug' if they seem to breeze through the daily grind taking it all in their stride (and celebrating every minute on their social media), while we're stuck feeling bored, tired, incompetent and inadequate in comparison. We seem to have an internal battle: desperately reaching for perfect supermum status – while secretly despising those women we feel are achieving it effortlessly.

> *'I just worry all the time that I'm not a good enough mum to her, that she is bored at home, that I'm not setting a good example, not making her happy. I want her to feel safe and happy and loved and wanted, but I don't know if I'm achieving that. I don't want her to be damaged by my inability to cope or respond appropriately to the more challenging bits of motherhood. I ultimately want her to have the happy childhood that I didn't. I feel I am failing.'*
>
> Sally, mum of one

Become a happier mum

Ultimately, we just want to be rewarded with an acknowledgement that we are doing a Good Job. But this kind of concrete reward system doesn't really happen as a mother in the way that it might have done in our educational or professional life before we became mums. We want our children to be 'safe, loved and happy', and all our actions are geared towards this one arguably intangible goal, so we often don't allow ourselves to recognise the achievement that *striving* for this goal in itself makes us pretty awesome mums.

This book will provide you with the tools to actively and positively move forward in softening into your mothering reality versus perfect ideal, and unlock the reasons why you got to where you are, by retracing the psychological steps to how your core belief system was formed and uncovering the factors that shaped your opinions and desires when it comes to your own mothering. Essentially, this book is here to help you feel OK about the fact that sometimes you think you're a crap mum.

We're all looking for some guidance occasionally. Six years into my motherhood adventure, it's still a constant source of amazement how incompetent my children can make me feel on a daily basis. How any poise and authority I might have wielded in a previous life or in my career is instantly thrown out the window when my son calls me a poo poo head and refuses to put his shoes on. When we feel helplessly incompetent, we lose trust in our instincts and can only seem to focus on what we're crap at: the cup becomes half emptied.

So through this book we're aiming to focus on your strengths, not your weaknesses. And to learn to see what is 'good enough' both individually *and collectively*, rather than us all perpetuating an unsustainable mythical supermum narrative. Do we all still believe that maternal perfection is achievable, despite the pressures of modern life? There's still arguably more societal pressure on mums than on dads to be the beacon of perfect light in the family, to be juggling all the family balls while also managing an immaculate blow-dry and a conference call.

Getting the hang of motherhood is less about controlling everything and more about realising what makes you happiest as a mother, and feeling confident enough to trust your instincts. With parenting, much of our underlying unhelpful thinking is a form of perfectionism, of aiming for ultra-high achievement. But it's hard to see it for what it is, as it manifests itself as extreme self-doubt.

We tend to think of perfectionism as an affliction that applies to highly strung Stepford mums who have perfect hair and could win *Bake Off* in their sleep. But it's just as likely to strike anybody who simply really cares about doing their best for their child (that'll be all of us, then?!). Once you accept that the anxiety and self-doubt are a manifestation of an unhelpful *mental habit*, it becomes easier to challenge them.

The Supermum Myth will tackle flash points at various mum-life stages – pregnancy, post birth, the toddler tunnel through to school days, juggling work around all this – with quotes and experiences from mums throughout. We'll explore how you're feeling and the range of *what's totally normal emotionally*, hormonally, etc. for you at each of these phases. There are activities peppered throughout, utilising different therapies, with suggestions, tips and techniques on how to overcome obstacles, and negotiate difficult experiences and tricky feelings.

Case studies are included at various points throughout the book. This is a chance for you to see how everyone is facing struggles in some form, even if they appear to have it all sorted on the surface – we all have a back story. You might identify with what someone has been through, and it might help you to organise your responses to some of the things you have experienced. Or, simply, reading about someone else's experience is a way of understanding that we are all negotiating the obstacles in our way – there is no smooth supermum road.

The therapies, with Dr Rachel Andrew

This book is designed to be *used* by you. Everyone is different, and we want you to make this book your own. We want you to interact by taking part in the activities, and to truly learn from them: learn about yourself and the way that you think – and how you can change the way you think, feel and behave, especially if these are becoming overwhelmingly negative and unhelpful.

If you can put aside some time and energy to really focus on the therapy activities, you will start to see what is happening in your thought patterns and understand why. This is the first step towards changing. If you then use the techniques and strategies in the most helpful ways for you, you will start to see a change in mindset and feel empowered to make more diverse choices about how you want to act.

The Supermum Myth is intended to be a highly practical book. We will discuss key psychological theories to help you understand more about core beliefs, dominant narratives, thought processes and emotions. Throughout, there will be ideas for visualisations, cognitive challenges, dealing with body sensations, interpreting feelings, and managing your mood and your relationships.

There are activities for you to do at various points. You can use a notebook or your phone – although we would recommend using a notebook (any excuse for some lovely stationery) – to help you create time *and space* to explore complex thoughts and memories. It's also often more effective to be able to review your thoughts if you actually have them down in black and white. Quite back to basics! The activities throughout the book are drawn from a number of different therapies.

Cognitive Behavioural Therapy (CBT)

CBT is a talking therapy that can help you manage your problems by changing the way you think and behave. CBT is based on the concept that your thoughts, feelings, physical sensations and actions are interconnected, and that negative thoughts can keep you trapped in a vicious cycle. It aims to help you deal with overwhelming problems in a more positive way by breaking them down into smaller parts and changing negative patterns.

Unlike some other talking treatments, CBT deals mostly with your current problems rather than focusing more on historic issues. It looks for practical ways to improve your state of mind on a daily basis.

Dialectical Behaviour Therapy (DBT)

DBT is a type of talking therapy that was originally developed by an American psychologist named Marsha Linehan. It is based on CBT, but has been adapted to meet the particular needs of people who experience emotions very intensely. DBT is a skill-based therapy, full of helpful ideas about managing overwhelming emotions, coping with relationships and building assertiveness.

It is mainly used to treat problems associated with borderline personality disorder (BPD), such as self-medicating with alcohol or drugs to control emotions, and eating disorders. It has been shown to be effective in treating a wide range of other disorders too, such as depression and post-traumatic stress disorder (PTSD).

Eye Movement Desensitisation and Reprocessing (EMDR)

EMDR therapy suggests that the mind can in fact heal from psychological trauma much as the body recovers from physical trauma. This therapy uses bilateral stimulation of the brain to help us process difficult experiences. It was developed by Francine Shapiro, who discovered that when she moved her eyes from left to right while thinking about upsetting memories she began to feel relief.

EMDR states that when we experience trauma, these traumatic memories are stored in their original state with all the body symptoms, smells and feelings still attached. When we remember them, they are still as fresh as the day they happened. The natural information processing that we do day to day has been blocked for these experiences. Using the detailed protocols and procedures learnt in EMDR therapy training sessions, clinicians help clients stimulate their natural healing processes so that these experiences are processed and filed away in the same way as normal memories would be, without being so intense and vivid.

Family therapy

Family therapy, or family and systemic psychotherapy, helps people in a close relationship to help each other. It enables family members, couples and others who care about each other to express and explore difficult thoughts and emotions safely, to understand each other's experiences and views, appreciate each other's needs, build on strengths and make useful changes in their relationships and their lives. Individuals can find family therapy helpful, as an opportunity to reflect on important relationships and find ways forward. Family therapy is useful for children, young people and adults experiencing a very wide range of difficulties and issues.

Mindfulness

Mindfulness is a relaxing therapy that allows us to become more aware of ourselves by noticing the stream of thoughts, feelings and body sensations we experience on a day-to-day basis. It can help identify any negative patterns and signs of stress or anxiety, and in turn give you a set of skills that help you focus your attention and live your life in the present, rather than being distracted by worries about the past or the future.

Narrative therapy

Narrative therapy is a form of psychotherapy that refers to particular ways of understanding people's identities. It helps people identify their core values, and the skills and knowledge they have to live these values, so they can confront whatever problems they're facing – a way of challenging the dominant discourses that can shape people's lives in destructive ways. The therapy helps you create a *new narrative* about yourself, by investigating how you came to have these core values.

Narrative therapy seeks to be a respectful, non-blaming approach to counselling and community work, which centres people as the experts in their own lives. It views problems as separate from people and assumes people have many skills, competencies, beliefs, values, commitments and abilities that will assist them to reduce the influence of problems in their lives.

Solution-focused therapy

The solution-focused approach aims to help individuals, teams and organisations to break out of vicious problem-cycles and develop constructive, customised solutions.

It does this by asking questions, rather than 'selling' answers, listening for and reinforcing evidence of the strengths, resources and competence of individuals, working with what people *can* do, not what they can't, finding out what people are already doing that is helpful and exploring ways to amplify their strategies, focusing on the details of the solutions, not the problems, and developing action plans that work.

Transactional Analysis (TA)

Transactional Analysis is a talking therapy designed to explore an individual's personality and how this has been shaped by experiences – particularly those from childhood. This is achieved through skilful questioning and the use of various models, techniques and tools.

The therapist works collaboratively with the individual to identify what has gone wrong in their communication and provide opportunities for them to change repetitive, potential-limiting patterns.

TA therapists recognise that we all have the potential to live the life we want, rather than the life we are programmed to live. Sometimes, however, this potential is hindered by repetitive patterns or 'unconscious scripts' that stem from childhood decisions and teachings.

Will all the activities be useful for me?

A key part of the therapy process is to show that *beliefs are not facts*. By getting into the habit of understanding and then interrogating your thought patterns and beliefs you can use logic to challenge just how flawed some of them are. Then you can break free of their hold. It's important to note that the therapies are for you to *dip into*: it may be that not all therapies will resonate with you.

You need to be able to connect to the activity on a very personal level, and possibly some of them don't quite fit or work for you. That's totally normal, and simply a sign of being human; it's not a one-size-fits-all system, which is why we have chosen a multi-therapy approach for this book. Don't be disheartened if an activity doesn't resonate with you – instead persevere and find one that hits the right nerve.

1

GAAH! Destructive emotions: making friends with guilt, anger, anxiety, hate

Welcome to *The Supermum Myth*. This first chapter will take you through the emotional landscape that you might be trekking through as a mum, and help you to understand and negotiate this rocky terrain to ensure that you can find a healthy emotional balance.

Becoming a mother brings with it joy, love and laughter, not to mention an abundance of stickers, glitter, odd socks – and an inordinate amount of crumbs and raisins in the bottom of your bag. But something not really mentioned in the traditional parenting books is that it also brings into your life more awkward emotions that you might not be prepared for.

It's hard to feel like a perfect mother as you gnash your teeth and shout with rage when your child christens your new sofa with indelible marker pen, or as you genuinely want to tip your toddler out the window when they decide that sleep is for the weak.

Which destructive emotions am I talking about? First, the mother of all mum emotions: **guilt**. I don't think I've met a mum who doesn't feel this every single day, on some level, in some way. Close behind comes **anxiety**: present like an annoying house-party guest who lingers on the sofa the next day despite you cleaning up around them and suggesting wordlessly that they really should leave now.

This chapter will also explore a range of emotions that we don't hear much about in terms of being 'natural' mothering feelings: **anger** and **hate**, envy and even loss – those feelings that you might not admit freely to having because they don't seem nurturing or normal, and they make you think you're a terrible mother. In fact, all of these feelings are completely human and 'normal', and the key is bringing them into healthy balance by *noticing* when you're feeling them, and why.

Emotions serve a useful purpose – they are signals from our body for us to respond in a certain way; they are there to tell us something valuable and to galvanise a response. Understanding them a bit better can help us figure this out.

> 'We like to imagine that motherhood brings with it a bottomless well of kindness and patience and generosity of spirit. But although being a mother brings out the very best of ourselves, it also brings out the very worst. Because mothering means all-consuming love and incandescent rage, searing joy and head-bashing frustration.'
> Antonia, mum of three, doula and antenatal teacher

The early stages of motherhood present tricky circumstances for us to calmly regulate our emotions in. Suddenly we're plunged into a world where sleep is not a guaranteed state, and, for the initial period at least, we're experiencing every hour of the 24 in the day – not to mention the physical trials that we have to battle through at the start of the motherhood road.

Cee, a mum of two girls, told me that in those early days, 'at one point, I thought I was going to die as everything felt so blocked up with mastitis. I was also on iron tablets, as I became anaemic during pregnancy, which gave me constipation. I had a complete breakdown after being on the toilet trying to poo for about six hours. It was awful. Those first three months were the absolute worst.'

We have to put up with a load of physical stuff that is, let's face it, fairly hideous at times, while also grappling with our new housemate and doing our best to keep them alive. So it's not surprising that our own internal dialogue gets pushed down on the list of important things to look after.

Tiredness and hunger, for example, make it difficult for our bodies to regulate themselves – anyone who has had to chaperone a tired and hungry toddler home on public transport without any snacks to hand will know the true meaning of 'hanger' (hunger meets anger) at its most pure. It's the same for us – except society doesn't really condone adults flinging themselves onto the floor, limbs thrashing around with tearful snotty abandon.

We can feel the same level of emotional turbulence, but this thrashing tends to go on internally once we're past the socially acceptable public-meltdown stage. Once we have a sense of the triggers for these unwelcome emotions, we can begin to get a handle on them and learn strategies for getting through the day without getting to meltdown point. That's what this chapter is here to help you do.

Emotion is power

So often, the vocabulary surrounding the way we feel as mothers is inherently negative: 'emotional', 'neurotic', 'paranoid', 'oversensitive'. Without adequate positive vocabulary to describe how we're *naturally* feeling as mums, it's difficult not to label yourself in a negative way. To begin with, we need to see that emotions are not 'good' or 'bad'. They just are.

Thinking that an emotion is 'bad' usually leads either to us trying to suppress it or to whipping up more negative feeling around it: guilt, shame, anger and anxiety come and join the party whenever the distressing feeling surfaces. And this is what you call a vicious circle. Adding an extra layer of difficult feelings to an already troubling situation simply makes the crappy feeling more intense and makes you less resilient, less able to tolerate how it's making you feel.

On the whole, a distressing feeling can be managed – as long as you don't then feel guilty or anxious about feeling those emotions in the first place: 'I'm feeling *really anxious* as he was really clingy and upset last night, it's not like him'; 'I know I'm *totally worrying too much* but there's something up with her – she's not being her usual self'; '*I felt so angry* when that woman on the bus made that comment about me bottle feeding – it's none of her business'; 'I'm *just feeling really emotional*, ignore me – I'm really tired'.

We continually invalidate our emotional state by suppressing, undermining or ignoring our emotions, when actually they are a powerful sign of mothering strength and instinct: of being a brilliant and caring mum; of noticing changes in your child's behaviour and knowing that these changes are worthy of note; of knowing that what you're doing is the right thing for *your* child; of realising that you're exhausted and actually you do need to be looked after a bit by the people around you. *Being emotional is a sign of Mum Power.*

Heightened emotions are proof that we are brilliant mothers, reacting to the greater demand on our ability to protect those important to us. That additional anxiety, the worry, the guilt are all sent to us for a purpose. The skill we need to unlock is being able to notice when we are most experiencing these emotions in undiluted thrashing-toddler form, and breaking down the messages they are trying to send us. Once we become our own emotional detectives and understand the purpose of the emotion, we can begin to focus on changing our response to it.

Charting your emotional landscape

We are often muddling along day to day in a kind of survival mode, mentally ticking off functional to-do lists and going through motions, getting through the week on autopilot: find shoes, find PE kits, make sure you don't leave one of your children in the supermarket, remember dentist appointments, buy nappies. This means that life can potentially pass you by – you're present but not really living the moment. On some days you might even be wishing the day away ('how can it still be four hours until bedtime, how, how??'). Then there's the 'bed dread' of the carnage of bedtime every night.

You might look back at your mothering experiences and feel that months, years even, were lived in a bit of a fog. In that kind of emotional framework, unhelpful feelings and thoughts have free rein to rummage around in your brain with impunity, as if you've left your front door wide open and allowed anyone from the street to wander in and take up residence in the spare room.

From here on, you can, with the help of this book, commit to *noticing* where you are mentally day to day: learn how to chart your emotional waters and begin to understand how you got there. The range of therapies and activities will give you the skills to learn *how* you can begin to notice when you are experiencing these emotions that you feel are negative, and learn how to make them positive.

> *'Motherhood kind of hit me like a car – I was floored, confused, guilty and highly, highly anxious.'*
>
> Amy, mum of two

The emotional rollercoaster

We need to learn how to balance these challenging feelings if they are becoming too dominant in our day and making us feel out of kilter. The emotional range that we feel as mums can mirror the pure, undiluted emotions that we experienced in our own childhood.

When you're dealing day to day with furious terrible-two outbursts about dinner being served on the wrong colour plate, or finding yourself in the midst of a volcanic pre-teen outburst about the unfairness of having to do homework, it's not always surprising that this heightened level of emotion starts to rub off on you a little bit. Plus, there is the simple intensity of your love for your child, which can be terrifying, heavily laced with fear, anxiety and anger.

This turbulent range of feelings may never have been the case in your mental landscape before your children were on the scene. It can be a positive thing: life is now in technicolor; there's a richness to the emotional tapestry that might have actually been missing before having children.

But the downside is that it's like riding white-water rapids if emotions start to get the better of you. Certain emotions can feed off the chaos – which can be overwhelming and make us feel very low. You might feel slightly ashamed as a mother if the prevailing feeling in your day is one of irritation, or weariness, or wanting to silently escape out the bathroom window into the night, rather than solidly overwhelming love.

> *'I never thought I'd be the kind of mum who would be almost desperately counting the minutes down until my partner walks in the door at the end of the day so that I could hand the baby over and escape to the loo for five minutes' peace.'*
>
> Kathryn, mum of two

The purpose of emotions is to *communicate* to you and to *motivate* actions and behaviour. To alert you to react. In this way, emotions function kind of like an alarm, to make sure you pay attention to events that may be important. It might sometimes be an annoying buzzy alarm way too early in the morning, but it's there for a reason. Identifying these *functions* of emotions, especially when they are unwanted emotions, is an important first step towards being able to change your reactions to them. *In a nutshell: you can form an alliance with the frenemy emotions.*

First, here's an exercise in learning how to identify your feelings. Developing this skill of self-awareness will gradually allow you to be more able to regulate your emotions and avoid emotional overwhelm.

Your emotional team

Think of emotions as being a team, your colleagues. In any good team, there need to be good communication lines set up between each member, with everyone taking on an even workload.

Is there a snippy member of the team who gets the others down and isn't a great team player, either hogging the workload and doing it badly, or not doing enough?

You need to learn how to be a good manager, and bring balance into the team so that all members are working to the same goal: being a calmer, happier mum.

Who is on your team?

1. Have a think and really explore how you feel on an average day – maybe choose a day when you know things aren't quite going to your best parenting plan to give you a real view of whether your emotions are your cheerleaders or rivals.

2. Now take a notepad and list the emotions that you feel make up your team in your day-to-day emotional landscape: is it anger, fear, worry, sadness …? Consider the following questions.

   • What is the role of each emotion? *What* is it trying to communicate to you?

   • *How* is it communicating this to you? Think about body feelings, thoughts and actions – e.g., when I feel anxious I notice my shoulders become tense and I breathe shallowly. I start to allow my thoughts to mushroom into worst-case scenarios.

3. You are on your own side. Stand in your own corner, and then try checking out your facts to see whether acting on your (very valid) emotions at that time is in your best interests.

This activity will help you to recognise your feelings. Once you know how you are feeling and why, remember to validate how you feel. Tell yourself, 'I can understand why I feel that way' or 'I have every right to feel as I do.' The exercise is about **recognising**, **validating** and then **checking**.

Remember, we only want to regulate or manage those emotions *that are not serving us best*, the team members that are spending their day browsing the internet and wasting office time rather than getting the job done.

Now that you've made your list of which emotions seem to make their presence felt in the most destructive ways, we can go through and look at strategies for bringing them into balance.

Keep revisiting your list as you go through this chapter, and see whether you can have more understanding of why and how you experience these emotions. Noticing is the first step to being able to change, and keeping a notepad to log these feelings, moods and emotions is an important way of doing this.

Guilt

So, hands up, who has felt any mum guilt today? Are you feeling guilty now for sitting down with a cup of tea and reading this book rather than putting on a load of washing/doing something more useful/ walking the dog? Guilt is a ubiquitous hashtag in our mum lives – the constant white noise behind most of our waking thoughts and decisions.

'I feel guilty about everything ALL THE TIME. Guilty even, sometimes, for just my thoughts. Guilty about having had gestational diabetes, guilty about needing an assisted delivery, guilty that I couldn't breastfeed, guilty that when I did establish it I then chose to combine feed; it goes on and on and on.'

Debbie, mum of two

So, what *is* guilt? Why do we experience guilt? Guilt is a powerful feeling that you have done, or intend to do, something very wrong, and have gone against your core values. Guilt is a true violation of what you feel is the correct order of things. Guilt is something that Lady Macbeth should have felt in spades, as then she might have thought twice about what she was getting her husband to do.

So the essence of *true guilt* is very targeted and distilled, to prevent you from performing future violations of such a terrible nature. Experiencing true guilt from having done something properly wrong is not ignorable, and tends to lead to action: taking responsibility and making amends. This is different from *mum guilt*, which is generally let loose willy-nilly like a happy Labrador in a field of rabbits.

Mum guilt is a *feeling* that simply lingers and hovers around, like your weird uncle at Christmas, rather than leading to any positive action. Have a think. What do you feel most guilt about on a day-to-day basis? Childcare/working? Spreading yourself evenly between siblings? Having/wanting 'me time'? Not doing 'enough' compared to other mums? Not baking enough biscuits or making enough models of spaceships from cereal cartons and loo rolls? Finding and eating some of your child's leftover Easter chocolate with your evening glass of wine? (That last one is totally acceptable behaviour and in my view should be encouraged.)

'I feel guilty more often than I can even number. When I pack my son off to school even when he says he's feeling poorly, because I need to get to work. When I always miss sports days and assemblies. The rising guilt about not being there for an old friend whose father is seriously ill … or just for any friends at all, because there never seems to be time to have an hour for a proper, uninterrupted conversation; the guilt that the house is always a mess … well, every single moment there is probably some guilt in there somewhere about something.'

Olivia, mum of three

Emotional labour

Mum guilt is an everyday trending hashtag on twitter. There are countless articles in magazines and websites about overcoming mum guilt. There are no doubt more than a handful of 'guiltymother' blogs and Instagram handles.

You don't really hear dads being associated with 'dad guilt' in quite the same all-pervasive way. How do dads cope with these emotions?

It might simply be a societal/cultural thing – as yet there is no superdad myth being perpetuated, but once truly flexible working is available and dads can take on a fully balanced and participative part of family life, might they too experience exactly the same emotional spectrum about it? Or is it simply that dads are very different in the way that they compartmentalise emotions and action? Are they just silent? Do they block it out more? Is it something they transfer to their partners ('I know the children are in good hands')? Can they rationalise it more?

On the whole, working or not, it is still the mother who takes on board much of the 'emotional labour' of the family. There are exceptions, of course – things are changing for a lot of families, and dads are absolutely more integrated into the throbbing hub of the family nowadays than they have ever been in previous generations.

By emotional labour I mean not just the housework/cooking/food shopping, which *tends* to fall to the mum in the house as a general stereotype, but the arranging of childcare, remembering of birthday presents and parties, of dental appointments, parents' evenings. The shoe buying and the cake-sale baking (or, ahem, supermarket cupcake dash ...). The immunisations. The assemblies. The permission forms for school trips. The oh-bollocks-is-it-World-Book-Day-today last-minute costumes.

It is still generally expected that Mum will be the person who leaves her job to take full maternity leave to care for a new baby, rather than it being societally acceptable that the dad might consider/want/even be able to do it. All of the minutiae of family life – the things that bob about as the tide takes them, racing like Pooh sticks – are generally held onto in the minds of the women steering the family boat.

With all this minutiae lies the awareness that there is *more that you should be doing* to be present, what might slip by the wayside if you do need to take your focus somewhere else. In focusing on so much detail, you're aware of what there is to be let go of if you were to devote 'too much' time or energy to yourself and your work/relationships/fun and lose track of even one part of this essential family admin.

Notice if you're wearing your guilt like a badge of honour – 'at least I feel guilty as it means I'm not a terrible mother who doesn't care', *'at least I feel bad* about not being perfect'. Why do you need to feel bad? Is it not better for your child, and, let's face it, for you, if you don't constantly feel bad? Would it really be a catastrophic failure if your child arrived at school without cupcakes for the cake sale?

I hereby ask you to try to cultivate, on just a small level, the glorious art of not giving a f*ck; soften into an imperfect scenario; let one of your plates slow its spinning. What would really, truly happen if there were no cakes from you for the cake sale? Possibly less money for the thing they're raising for ... well, donate a few extra quid. Job solved. Guilt, be gone.

No one would actually notice – your cakes are not conspicuous by their absence. That tiramisu from the professional chef mum in 4G was always going to be better anyway. Whenever you do feel you've allowed a plate to stop spinning, rather than catastrophise and let the guilt in, try to focus on what has been achieved, what you have successfully completed. *It's good enough to be good enough.*

Source of guilt: I left my toddler at the childminder, crying and unhappy.

Achievement: Going to work: making money, creating more sense of self, using your brain, having me time (e.g. going to the loo on your own), being able to be more sane and present for her when you are with her.

Source of guilt: I ruined my first child's third birthday party because I ended up going into labour with his brother.

Achievement: Er ... you had a baby. And thereby created a means of him developing strategies for resolving conflict within a safe environment, and of helping him to understand that essentially life isn't fair, which will benefit him for his whole life. Plus it's probably a great story to be recounted at family gatherings forever.

Source of guilt: I didn't take my second baby to any baby groups or classes because I really preferred to hang out with her in cafés that I wanted to go to while she couldn't move, and enjoy this blissful time before she started wrecking stuff. And that means she didn't have any friends as a toddler compared to toddlers of other mums I know, so I'm sure I've stunted her social development forever.

Achievement: You spent quality one-to-one time with your child. Toddlers aren't very good at having friends anyway – they tend to invade their personal space, pull clumps of hair out, poke fingers in eyes and claim beloved possessions as their own. Children learn by observing: she'll have watched her older brother's relationships and hero-worshipped him, and no doubt have mucked in with his friendships. Preschool/school is really where it's at in terms of developing long-term social skills away from your gaze. Far better to have spent time with you happy and relaxed drinking coffee than sitting singing *Wind the Bobbin Up* and wanting to gouge your own eyes out with boredom.

Source of guilt: I can't afford all the stuff that my children need – that all the other kids seem to have.

Achievement: *You* are pretty much all they need: your time, your focus, your energy, your love, your curiosity, your determination, your resilience, your touch. You can't give them this fully unless you are kind enough to yourself to see how brilliant you are and what a hero you are in your children's eyes. You are your child's entire universe. You are enough, honestly. The rest is basically just stuff.

'I completely failed at breastfeeding and gave up trying after only a week. Even writing that makes me feel guilty now.'
Elizabeth, mum of two

So let's try to get to grips with our mum guilt. Here are a couple of lovely activities that are worth trying.

ACTIVITY

Write an advert for the real (imperfect) supermum

Get yourself a notepad and a pen. Allow yourself 15 *guilt-free* minutes, with a cup of tea or a glass of wine. You are going to advertise for the best mum you could possibly imagine for your children.

1. Before you put pen to paper, think about the types of things that you know your child really appreciates, as well as the things that you would ideally love if you were that 'perfect' mum that you have a bit of a mum crush on at playgroup. What kind of mum powers would you want from the ideal candidate? Really have

a think about the qualities that you feel *your* children need and would benefit from.

2. Now write the advert in whatever style you like, highlighting the top things that you would want to have as skills and attributes.

You could use a humorous style, as in the following example.

Looking to hire the best mum for Wilf and Ruby.

Must love rough and tumbling, cheese sandwiches and running around barefoot in the mud. Applicants should be able to speak in a convincing dinosaur voice, be interested and passionate about marine biology (not bored of watching Octonauts on repeat) and able to at least attempt to make jetpacks out of loo rolls. Shouters need not apply.

Or, if you don't want to be jokey, you could write your advert as a list of things you truly would want in an ideal world for your perfect parent to be:

- a good listener
- always calm and patient
- good at crafts
- cooks healthy food
- does not lose temper
- fair and balanced
- always there to offer cuddles and kisses
- sporty and game for a laugh.

This activity usually leads to two different discoveries. First, you might find that your ideal is often unrealistic, but that the process has allowed you to create a sort of audit about what is important to you as a mother, which is quite useful for noticing when you're not acting as 'perfectly' as you might like. Second, you might notice that you are actually achieving way more 'perfection' than you thought, and that your children's needs are not always as complex as life makes them seem.

You can also do this activity with your children, although ideally you would get someone else to do it with them in your place – especially if they're a bit older – so they don't have the self-consciousness of being with you while you're asking them, 'Sooo, what would the perfect mum be for you then, hey, hey?'

1. Ask your children to write their own advert for a perfect mum.

2. Ask them to write what they love most about you, their actual mum.

This can be an emotional activity, as often children will ask for much less and are simply not bothered about the things we are, so it can sharpen our focus as to what is important to them. Asking them what they love about their mum can help you see what it is about you that they feel is important – and it can be quite funny to see the silly things that mean so much to your children. This can help you realise that sometimes in life it really is the little things that matter.

I did the second activity with my eldest son, who is five – as a caveat, I can't be sure that there wasn't biscuit-based coercion involved.

Maurice said: 'Your hair is soft and I love cuddling you. I love your lullabies. I want to keep you forever.' Aahh. Sigh .... He then did also say that I am the best because I buy him presents, asked, 'Is it Christmas soon?' and demanded the new Go Jetters Jet Pad toy, so let's move swiftly on rather than dwell on the irony coming from me of the 'you are enough' assertion from earlier on, shall we?

One thing is for sure. The very fact that you have picked up this book and chosen to try to do something to empower yourself and make your mental landscape more positive for you and your children is proof enough that you have no reason to ever feel guilty. You can dump the guilt.

Anger

Now, I don't know about you, but pre-kids I was a pretty serene person. The kind of person who might simmer inwardly, but who wasn't often visited by rage – and I certainly wasn't prone to losing my rag and shouting in the middle of the Science Museum, surrounded by people gawking. It's not just my children who elicit anger from me; it might be my partner, or the mum who insists on telling me about her child who sleeps so perfectly when I'm in the cold dark depths of sleep-deprivation torture, or someone else's child in the playground being a complete arse ...

Since having my second child and therefore having less time, less energy, less patience, less sleep, there is more often than not an audible 'FFS!!!' or strange animal growling noise lurking dangerously near the surface. I was quite alarmed by how my first suddenly became a source of extreme anger after my second was born, how my fuse suddenly seemed to be lit and burning out rapidly, how quickly my responses escalated to volcanic. I definitely felt uncomfortable with this, and its effects on my mental health and my relationship with my poor eldest, who up until then hadn't ever had to deal with a particularly shouty mumma.

> 'I have a terrible temper and sometimes my children bear the brunt of that, so when that temper is triggered, I have often questioned my ability to be a good mother.'
>
> Hannah, mum of two

Anger is there to *provoke our response* to the blocking of important goals or activities, or to an imminent attack on ourselves or on people important to us. It focuses us on self-defence, mastery and *control*. Control – that's the biggie, isn't it? I don't know about you, but I feel anger rising when we need to get out of the house as we're late and I've lost my keys, I inexplicably can't collapse the fricking buggy, the children are fighting and refusing to put their coats on ... or maybe it's at the end of a testing no-napping-toddler, all-of-the-above day and your husband comes home, just missing a crazy bedtime, and enquires why you haven't put any washing on. Those are the moments when I tend to want to suddenly throw my hands up and shout STOP THE WORLD I WANT TO GET OFF!!! Or something with a bit more profanity in it. If I'm over tired, I get to that shouty rageful place much faster.

Let's try to notice how and when anger comes to visit you.

Mood dump

ACTIVITY

Take your notebook. You can even get busy with some doodling and pictures here – it doesn't have to be all words.

1. Visualise yourself in an actual rubbish tip. What are the things that are dragging you down/squashing you/piling on top of you?

   Imagine each of your stresses as bits of rubbish, and name each stressor:

- the school run
- my husband playing football
- making packed lunches
- baby bottles
- getting the bag packed.

Sometimes we feel frustrated and overwhelmed and simply don't understand why as we've never questioned it, let alone looked at it in black and white. Thinking about the *detail* of your life and stresses focuses you on the things you don't normally notice when you're living through them. When you write them down, there might be a whole page of stuff that anyone would feel overwhelmed by.

Just seeing what's there and having a good rummage is often a good first step. Once you have a concrete representation of the things that are weighing you down and causing you anger, you can begin to think about ways that you can take steps to maybe change your routine or ask for help.

2. Show the list to your partner; see whether a discussion about it provokes any useful suggestions for changing morning routines/bedtime routines/whatever your needling areas are. Even sometimes putting organisational strategies into place, like a trip to IKEA for a shoe rack so all the shoes are sitting waiting by the door every morning, can remove a whole load of emotional rubbish being dumped on you.

The shouting trap

I never used to be a shouty person so it makes me feel crappy to shout, it doesn't feel like 'me'. Shouting at your child and then feeling mum guilt about it is a really fun mixture. This anger/guilt cocktail is ultimately positive, as it usually makes us keen not to have future outbursts because they made everyone feel a bit rubbish – remember: emotions are there to provoke responses, *actions* – and that intention shows you are a good mother and mindful of the result of your mood on your child's emotions. Being angry shows our children that this is a normal human emotion. The trick is also showing them how to deal with it in a healthy fashion.

Make sure you notice the balance and fairness – if you (in calm times) tell your child off for showing their anger with another child/with their teacher/with life in general, be mindful that actually they may be mirroring the way that you deal with similar stressors. Make it honest and open. Allow there to be an acknowledgement when you lose your cool, and apologise for it if you know an apology is necessary: 'Mummy's just feeling really tired today and I got cross because you wouldn't put your socks on [silently in your head: and were being a little bugger].'

> *'Being patient and firm, while seeing things from the child's point of view to understand their behaviour, is what I would like to do but often doesn't happen and I often end up just shouting or dismissing and then feel bad about it later. When I lose it and flip out – usually when I am particularly sleep deprived or stressed for other reasons – I might take it out on the boys – as they are the only ones around and causing extra stress.'*
>
> Elizabeth, mum of two

The psychologist Donald Winnicott, who developed the concept of the good-enough mum that we'll talk a bit more about in Chapter 6 on page 137, believes that anger from your children shows ultimately that they believe strongly that you are there for them and it shows their attachment: '... when children hit and scream their hate at us ... anger is an essential component of love, and indifference is its true opposite.'

Being open and honest shows them that it's OK to have these emotions, we're all fallible, it passes, you can express how you feel and most importantly *it doesn't mean a lack of love*. Remember anger is a passing state, so don't empower it by holding on to it and allowing it to build. It's a storm. There are always calmer waters ahead.

> *'I think I'd definitely be a better mother if I didn't lose my temper so much.'*
>
> Kate, mum of three

Remember you are *always modelling behaviour* for your children, perhaps even more so in these intense moments of heightened emotion than at any other time. They are continually observing you and learning skills of dealing with situations from you. If you teach them that shouting without explanation is the way that we deal with things, then that's the way it's going to be for them too. They become little mirrors.

> *'I see my four-year-old telling her toys/little brother off, and it's scary how she wags her finger and uses phrases which I know come directly from my mouth. Horrible phrases like "you are being an absolute nightmare, I've had enough of you". I hate seeing it, it makes me feel really ashamed.'*
>
> Alex, mum of two

> *'I get so angry with my boys. But I can see that shouting just makes them switch off, so we're in this shout-shout-nothing-changing cycle.'*
>
> Charlotte, mum of twins

Anger expressed in other ways

Mothering is stressful, and utterly knackering. And you do need to give yourself a break when you lose your cool occasionally. But I also want you to take a good honest look and notice if you're sometimes allowing hostility to be shown in other ways, which can be more damaging than letting it all out with a shout. Do you ever express your hostility through the tone of your voice: sarcastic or venomous? I know I have. Being quite mean with the things you say when you're feeling really rattled?

These are the things that you have to *notice* and be really honest with yourself about if you see it as a pattern within your behavioural backpack, as they are the things that are less easy for a child to process: there is obviously hostility, but it isn't overt and is harder to understand – yet it will definitely make an imprint on their minds.

> *'Sometimes I really want to scream and shake her she makes me so mad, and then I just feel so shit and get angry with myself; it's not her fault, she's only six ... I'm the grown-up. But I'm just so bloody exhausted and sometimes don't have enough energy for her constant demands.'*
>
> Katherine, mum of two

Notice if you express your anger in other, physical, ways: grabbing, pushing, manhandling into buggy/clothes. (Although I concede it is impossible to get a rigid tantruming toddler into a buggy without some element of manhandling.) Once, when my eldest was three, he was kicking me and fannying around so much when we were trying to get his shoes on that I put him down on the sofa and walked away as I needed to escape to another room to get away from him and my mounting anger. He shouted after me, 'Mummy, why did you throw me on the sofa?' It forced me to realise I had allowed an unhealthy rage to take over in that moment.

Extreme anger or other intense emotions can be like falling into a choppy sea, where you have absolutely no control over which direction you will go or whether you'll be taken under by the swell. Your reasonable mind doesn't have a chance to surface and moderate the influence of the emotional mind. Understanding that, and being able to throw yourself a line to lift yourself out, is key.

Visualise a lifeboat throwing you a breathing line. Breathe: take a 7-second in-breath, and an 11-second out breath. Think 7–11, 7–11. Pause. Notice if you are thinking or even saying out loud to your child, 'Stop being so bloody childish!' And remind yourself that, well, they *are* the child. Repeating the mantra, 'I am the adult, I am calm' can help. Calm.

Visualise still, peaceful waters. Create a physical distance between yourself and your child if necessary in those moments, allow a space for the anger to dissipate into. Or, alternatively, do the opposite: squeeze the anger out of its space, hug it out. A hug is *always* a good thing to do in almost any circumstance. Perhaps not during chats with the headteacher though ...

Anger can feel like a scary emotion, and can really affect your interaction with your children. It can become a negative pattern of behaviour if you don't really notice why you're feeling it so intensely and try to remove the triggers, or reframe your response to them. Share with your child why you're feeling angry – 'I'm sorry, I'm feeling angry right now because you deliberately pushed your bowl of Cheerios onto the floor' – so that they can appreciate that ultimately it's not about how you feel about them personally.

Allow them to make the connection between your actions and your emotions, and to learn positively from you by seeing that anger can visit but that it doesn't have to take complete control. There's no need to be perfect, if perfect to you means not showing signs of difficult emotions.

Buddhism has some great teachings for dealing with anger. Buddha was, after all, the most serene of chaps, so we could all learn a lot from him. Sarah Napthali, in *Buddhism for Mothers*, recommends trying the following techniques in moments when anger takes over.

1. Dwell on the positive.
2. Consider the results of your thoughts.
3. Distract yourself.
4. Consider the alternatives: why am I angry, is it inevitable? Remember *we create our own reality*. Second guess your thoughts a bit, switch your automatic response on its head.
5. Use your willpower: when you feel anger mounting, say, 'Let go. Enough. Calm.'

> '*I love my son to the moon and back, but he winds me up so much that it can scare me that in the moment I want to pinch him, or squeeze his arm really hard so that he can feel it and it'll shock him out of being such a drama queen. I've never acted on those physical impulses, but I've never felt anger like it and it always shocks me to realise, later, that he's pushed me to that point.*'
>
> Angela, mum of three

A last word: swearing – it can be healthy and it definitely helps let it all out, but it can be a real sign of losing control. My blood ran cold when my three-year-old corrected me one day after a pavement versus buggy board altercation, saying 'it's not a "f*cking buggy", Mummy, it's a "buggy".' Red face. Keep it in check. Keep it for 'you' – escaping to the loo and silently shouting, 'f*ck, b*gger, b*llocks' to yourself really does have a cathartic effect.

Anxiety

When you become a mum you suddenly become porous – so much more sensitive to what can go wrong, hazards, diseases, evils, and the ills that are present in society. Or, looking closer to home, you might simply feel 'blimey I know *nothing* about children' and search out certainty in parenting manuals so that the 'experts' can tell you what to do, drawing you away from your instincts and making you prone to anxiety about getting it 'wrong'.

Anxiety organises our responses to threats to our life, health and wellbeing, focuses on our *escape from danger*. It encompasses feelings of unease, worry and fear – and this includes both the emotions and the *physical sensations* we might experience when we are worried or nervous about something.

Challenge your thoughts

Don't believe every thought you think. Our automatic thoughts pop in without us consciously summoning them. That doesn't mean that they are fact, yet we tend to believe them as such. You have the power to either welcome thoughts in or ask them to leave. Imagine them like sales purchases – you can take them back if they don't suit you. Or think of them as clouds in the sky, passing through, rather than inviting them to linger and become storm clouds. Anxiety makes us feel that the world is very threatening. It's important to aim for a healthy balance between what's real and what's your anxiety simply making stuff up. We'll talk about this all of more in the next chapter.

Self-care habits (see pages 106–110) form an important part of addressing your symptoms of anxiety in the long term. Self-care doesn't necessarily mean withdrawing and finding time for 'you' alone, it also means connecting with people: talking with friends honestly about issues that are troubling you. Be open if you are experiencing more than a sprinkle of anxious thoughts and feelings in any given day. If your anxiety starts to become too dominant in your emotional 'team' (see page 19), think about having a chat with your GP.

> *'I can go quickly from calmly walking down the supermarket aisle with my child to visualising her being abducted from underneath my nose. It's utterly exhausting.'*
>
> Becky, mum of one

Figures from the NHS (2016) show that anxiety is on the rise, particularly among young women. As a mum, you're more likely to suffer from anxiety if you have suffered miscarriages, had a traumatic birth, or if you had problems with fertility. Or it may simply have come out of the blue, possibly a symptom of postnatal depression, or a result of being physically and emotionally depleted by your birthing and mothering experience, and losing some of your resilience.

Anxiety and your body

Anxiety is a *normal healthy reaction*. It happens to everyone in times of danger or in worrying situations. When we feel anxious, a chain of hormonal responses happens in our bodies: the 'fight, flight or freeze' response – designed to prepare us to fight the perceived danger, get the hell out of there and run away from it, or, perhaps more commonly in its modern incarnation, freezing and being incapable of doing anything.

When we find ourselves in what we perceive as a 'dangerous' situation, a hormone called adrenaline is released into the bloodstream. Our breathing rate increases. Our heart rate increases, to pump the additional oxygen and adrenaline round the body quickly. With all this increased activity, our body heats up so we might sweat. We need to go to the toilet more frequently. Yes, you're right, these feelings are all commonly associated with a trip to softplay with your kids.

Imagine the primitive caveman threatened by a wild animal: in order not to be munched by the sabre-toothed cat, he needs to be able to scarper as quickly as he can. Being alert and able to flee at any given moment was what enabled prehistoric man to survive. We still have this exact same fight-or-flight hormonal and physical response to perceived threats and danger, although we now more than likely experience it in non-life-threatening situations, such as the queue in Tesco. In modern life, our perception of 'danger' can escalate out of proportion, leaving us feeling like crap, or gradually becoming scared of and avoiding the activities that we used to be carefree about, because everything is veiled with a cloak of fear.

Disturbing thoughts

This is a common anxiety symptom for mums, as quite simply we become extremely sensitive to any potential hazards that might harm our babies from birth. You might be on constant high alert, thinking that something terrible is going to happen, seeing all the worst-case scenarios in hidden corners. You might be totally unaware that you have a habit of catastrophising, and these thoughts are causing you to feel constantly anxious or frightened, and this mushrooms out of all proportion until you're backed into a corner.

'I think I was unprepared for just how vulnerable my newborn was. I drove myself mad with seeing dangers anywhere and everywhere: knives in the kitchen, pillows that could smother her, even hugging her too tight I was worried about. I would vividly imagine dropping her as I walked down the stairs. I still find now that I can almost "see", flashing in front of my eyes, my children scooting straight into the road in front of a bus, and it makes me physically shudder.'

Ellie, mum of two

'I find it hard to stop worst-case scenarios developing in my head. For example, if I hear about a rape case on the news, it makes me initially worry about the world my daughter is growing up in. Then without being able to catch it, it develops into catastrophising thoughts to the point where I'm adamant that my daughter will never be allowed to go to university/leave home/be away from me ever again so that I can protect her always. If my partner tells me I'm being ridiculous, I've actually banished him to the spare room for days without speaking to him ... it's not realistic, and it's exhausting, but it happens, on some level, every week.'

Alison, mum of one

Once you begin to notice and recognise this thought behaviour, and realise that you're believing your thoughts as if they were true, you can learn to challenge them (see Chapter 2, The Thought Police, page 43). Concentrate your mind on the truth in front of you: on what is actually happening here and now, rather than what you think might happen, and this will help you feel less anxious. Or, if you are actually in the hell of softplay feeling anxious, concentrate on the relaxing cup of tea that you will have when you get home ...

'Breastfeeding was my anxiety tripwire. I obsessed over who was and wasn't breastfed in my friendship group and then

drilled down on their health history. I heard song lyrics like the Beatles' "Lady Madonna" (baby at your breast ...) and felt like I was the only one in the world who couldn't breastfeed – I felt like a biological freak. It even got to the point where I believed my daughter wasn't a "real" baby – she had formula and therefore wasn't as good as other, breastfed babies. Without other friends in the same situation to put it into perspective, I was a total nutcase.'

Amy, mum of two

Avoidance behaviour

When my first was a tiny baby, he was an angry little soul and liked to scream, a lot. I basically turned into a hermit and withdrew entirely from 'normal' activities outside the house. No public transport, no cafés, no supermarkets. I spent a lot of time walking the buggy alone around the park. I didn't leave my postcode for seven weeks.

Looking back, I can see very clearly that my heightened anxiety about potentially dealing with his constant crying in public made me simply avoid ever going out in public. Although avoidance may seem like a good solution at the time, it's not really because the more you avoid a situation or problem, the more frightening it then becomes – and with me as an example, this can lead to horrendous social isolation and loneliness, which only exacerbates anxiety.

Modern-day anxiety is a festering fear that inhibits you from living your life freely and contentedly. You might worry that if you were to put yourself in the feared situation, something dreadful would definitely happen – you might 'lose it', the world will fall apart. In fact, what usually happens when you face your fear is that although you may have to deal with anxious thoughts initially, the fear reaches a peak, then fades away. Facing up to a feared situation is called 'exposure'. Over time, repeated exposure has the effect of lessening the fear. If nothing else, it can show you that it's not the end of the world if your baby screams endlessly on the bus; you lived through it and tomorrow is a new day. The world keeps on turning.

Calming the anxiety

ACTIVITY

Mindfulness and relaxation approaches go a long way to helping you manage anxiety in the moment, addressing your physical response. Once you have calmed that, you can then focus on what works for you to calm the *causes* of your anxiety in a more thoughtful, adaptive way.

Coming back to the breath

This exercise is as simple as it sounds, and can be done anywhere ... even in softplay.

When you're feeling overwhelmed, take a moment to focus on your breathing, following the steps below.

- Take a long breath in through your nose, for 5 seconds. Breathe out through the lips as if you're trying to fog a window in front of you, for 6 seconds.
- Breathe in for 5, out for 7.
- Breathe in for 5, out for 8.
- Repeat until your exhalation is twice the length of your inhalation.
- Relax your jaw, your cheeks, your forehead.
- Soften your shoulders.
- Notice your spine: feel it lengthening and releasing your energy up.
- Do a scan of your body, fully noticing every part, down to each finger and each toe. Try to soften each part of your body as you focus on it.

There you go – calmness achieved.

How to make friends with anxiety

1. *Anxiety is a normal emotion, a purposeful feeling that ultimately aims to look after you and keep you/your child from harm. Look at your anxious thoughts, physical sensations and behaviour habits. Write them down. Each time you feel anxious, remind yourself that it is 'normal', 'healthy' and 'natural'. These words will gradually soften your perception of it.*

2. *Learn ways to relax and find flow.* Find ways of switching off your anxiety. Is your anxiety a cat with bristled fur, ready to pounce? See how you can get your cat to curl up and purr blissfully instead. Practise calm breathing and muscle relaxation. Calming activities could be colouring books (get yourself a lovely adult one full of beautiful serene designs rather than using your child's Peppa Pig one – but make sure your toddler doesn't claim it), yoga, music, drinking a nice gin …

3. *Feel your fear, and do it anyway.* Work out what kinds of situations you tend to avoid or cause you fear. Try to actually go towards these situations. I'm not talking about putting yourself in danger physically, ladies, but expose yourself to situations that normally you would allow yourself to run from without question. The idea is that you try to remain in the situation until your anxiety gives up and goes home. It's not the easiest road, but it does work in the long term for reducing symptoms of anxiety by ultimately making you realise that 'it's not that bad actually'.

ACTIVITY

Anxiety as a small child

Imagining anxiety as a little child will change the way you interact with it. It's the vulnerable, frightened bit in all of us that needs some hand-holding and encouraging in a calm, soothing tone.

- Don't shout at or threaten it, as this will only make it feel more scared.

- When you're feeling your body and mind symptoms of anxiety, imagine being your own coach; perhaps base this on someone you know – a school teacher, mentor, aunt or uncle or friend – and use their tone to say encouraging things like, 'I know you can do this', 'You have dealt with situations like this before', 'It's ok'.

Hate

Anyone who's ever had their baby woken by a careless doorbell knows the true meaning of hate. Hate is a complex and guilt-inducing emotion that often paradoxically only enters our lives after we become mothers, when we're supposed only to experience heightened states of love.

'I was having an argument with my nine-year-old daughter and she shouted that she hated me, and I felt like, at that moment, I hated her too. Thankfully I didn't actually say to her what I was feeling. I felt horrible afterwards when I had calmed down, totally ashamed.'

Rachel, mum of one

I went on a yoga retreat recently – a fully indulgent mum self-care strategy that I very much recommend – and met lots of interesting and inspirational women at various life stages. Some had small babies, others had grown-up children. All were from different countries, backgrounds and professional areas. One thing that came up in a particular detox-juice-fuelled bonding chat was that it was apparently common to have fleeting feelings of hatred for your partner, particularly when kids are thrown into the mix. What a relief – it's normal and doesn't necessarily have to signal anything terrible. But how do you deal with it and make sure it doesn't come out of balance?

'I sometimes catch myself feeling intense hate for my partner for having a life outside the home, for going out for drinks, for being a separate person whereas I feel like I've been completely consumed by small children. It's really destructive.'

Eleanor, mum of two

Sometimes we might not *like* our children/partner, but that doesn't mean that we don't always love them. However, you have to be mindful of when that balance is tipping and when you forget to 'see' those close to you anymore. With your children, that unconditional love is more of a given. They (probably) had residence in your womb for nearly a year, and were pushed out of your body with quite a lot of effort, either through the sunroof or the door. They have the whole of your soul invested in their wellbeing and are physical extensions of your heart, your skin. But for your partner, that unconditional love can become conditional quite easily once the exhaustion and monotony of parenthood kicks in. If you fall out of 'like' day to day, then, by degrees, over time you might start to empty out some of the love.

'If my partner calls me, having already missed the chaos of bathtime, and tells me that he's going for "a quick beer", and I know I've got to do another bedtime alone, I truly hate him.'

Jess, mum of two

Sarah Napthali's *Buddhism for Mothers* offers some great strategies for dealing with hatred creeping stealthily into your relationships. She talks about 'skilful behaviour reinforcing love', and 'unskillful behaviour' reinforcing a sense of disconnect, of separation.

Skilful behaviour: take an interest, give time and attention, praise each other. Stop, and realise – notice if your thought patterns or knee-jerk reactions are overwhelmingly negative when you consider your partner. If so, take some time to dwell instead on good qualities, perhaps the lovely things that you see reflected in your joint creation – your children.

These are simple steps, perhaps obvious – but very easy to let slide. Extreme exhaustion can result in destructive patterns within relationships, with your partner and with your children. But noticing it and taking small steps can ensure it doesn't become out of control.

Envy

Arguably the queen of all supermum unhelpful emotions is envy. We tend to impose supermum status on other mums because we compare ourselves unfavourably with them. Essentially, we 'want a bit of what she has' – or even if we hate the smugness of (what we perceive as) the perfect supermum, on some level this may be because she's demonstrating something that we feel we want to have/do/be. Do you ever suffer from the green-eyed monster – envy of the mum who seems to have it all, of the mum who is doing it much better than you, of the mum of sleeping children, of the mum with all the free time, of the mum with the great job/house/relationship/hair ...?

Envy organises our responses to others getting or having things we do not have – and focuses us on working hard to obtain these things. So, it *can* be a positive thing if it prompts you to strive harder for what you want. But it's easier to allow it simply to needle you and make you feel a bit crap. Choose which version of envy you prefer, and decide whether you are going to have productive envy or destructive envy.

Gratitude and intentions

1. Write a **Gratitude List**.

   - Take your notebook and write down five things that you are grateful for. It could be something intangible like your health, or the fact that it's sunny today, or something more concrete like the roof over your head.

   - Note down your mood.

   - Make a habit of writing your gratitude list every week, or even every day.

2. Then, create an **Intentions List**.

   - Again, these intentions could be concrete goals, such as 'new curtains in the living room', or intangible ones, such as 'to feel happier and healthier'.

   - Make sure that you write down a step that you're going to take to action your intention, e.g. 'save £20 every week for curtains', or 'start swimming'.

   - *Make it happen,* by putting steps in the diary that require you to take action. Review your intentions and your gratitude list on the same day every week.

Feelings of sadness and loss

One of the most difficult mum emotions is feeling an underlying sense of loss for who you used to be before you became a mum. We'll explore this in much more detail in Chapter 4, but for now just be reassured that it's part and parcel of the emotional tapestry of motherhood, and don't be ashamed if you feel sad. It's never a reflection of how much you love your children – more an affirmation of how much you love yourself.

Feelings of sadness are there to organise responses to the loss of something important, perhaps goals lost or not attained. They're sent to focus us on what we do value and love, as well as on *communicating to others that we need help.* That's crucial – if you're feeling a sense of sadness, invite someone over for a cup of tea and have a chat about it. Sadness is never something that should be left on its own, and by sharing it you'll lessen its heaviness – and you might find that others are feeling similar. Here's a lovely final activity for approaching these tricky feelings.

A letter to your pre-mum self

Write a letter to your pre-mum self, as if she were a long-lost friend.

- Say what you miss most about her and what she used to do.
- Share with her what you have now discovered about motherhood, both its joys and disappointments.
- Think of how you could bring the two of you back together again. Perhaps there are ways that you could meet up again; e.g. through a night out with friends, a music gig or a trip to the cinema – anything that fires your mojo up a bit more and makes you feel like 'you'.

These emotions are natural, and part of being a mum

We've learnt in this chapter that you *can* be an amazing mum and still feel the awkward emotions that make you feel like you're falling down somewhat in your perfect mum status. Reframing our relationship with these natural mothering, human, emotions is the first step to empowering yourself to feel like you can be the best mum, every day, for at least part of the day.

Just try to keep the 'FFS!!' under your hat as much as you can, even when you're under siege from mutant ninja preschoolers while all you want is to go the loo on your own.

'When I plan and things actually pan out as I planned, I feel amazing. Like a supermum. And if the kids acknowledge my success, that makes everything even better. Everything I do, I do for them.'

Cee, mum of two

2

The Thought Police: your core beliefs

In this chapter we're going to focus on your thinking patterns: noticing where your internal dialogue began, the repeated negative message you're sending yourself of 'failure', and how this informs your emotional and behavioural patterns; working out *how* you got to where you are in terms of the judgements you are making about yourself; and we'll practise tuning into your automatic thoughts so that you can question them, and build your resilience to perceived judgements from others.

There'll be exercises to enable you to reconcile any disparity between the mum you always thought you'd be and the (brilliant) mum that you actually are. Forgiving yourself any perceived 'failures' is the main aim here – breaking down the myth that there is a perfect ideal and that if you don't embody it you have failed.

Be your own thought detective

We need to begin by identifying how you arrive at your judgements of yourself and your assumptions about what others are thinking about you. Examine your thoughts: your automatic thought loop, the ones that pop into your head uninvited. These thoughts form a constant soundtrack in our heads – it's a familiar voice that is always there, so we never stop to question whether what we are thinking is actually *true*.

It's sort of like inviting anyone into your home who claims to be the gas man, simply trusting him without checking his identification badge. Well, you just wouldn't, would you – even if he had a really honest face? So do yourself the same courtesy – safeguard your wellbeing by second-guessing your honest-faced thoughts.

What are core beliefs?

Core beliefs are like an internal stone manifesto – a list of truths we think we know about ourselves, etched there permanently so we don't even think to reread or try to amend them. It's a bit like the chicken-pox scar on your cheek – you've never questioned it as it's part of you, and you don't remember a time when it wasn't there. Core beliefs just *are*.

They help us to predict what will happen and are the blocks that we build out of our experiences to make sense of our world: 'I am ...', 'I always ...', 'I'm the kind of person who ...', 'I never ...'. These core beliefs are formed in childhood, and our subsequent experiences develop them into ideas about:

- how we see ourselves, others and the world
- how we judge what we do
- how we view the future.

Even if they are negative and a bit unhelpful, we tend to view our beliefs as *fact* – so we never think to stop and question them. Say one of your core beliefs is 'I am unlovable': accepting this as truth can lead to distress if you feel that Nancy's mum at school doesn't like you. If your core belief is 'I am unlovable', your *assumption* would then be, 'If I am not liked by everyone, that means I must be unlovable.'

Core beliefs put a spin on *the way we see a situation* – like putting on a pair of 'unlovable' glasses. Because we *see ourselves* as unlovable, we interpret Nancy's mum not saying hello one day as a personal slight, and as *proof* that 'She doesn't like me.' There might be loads of other reasons for it, but we can't see them. You are tuning in to the evidence that supports your belief that 'I am unlovable'. Even if that person is not 'important' to you – perhaps you don't actually particularly like her either – your core belief underpinning your responses overrides any rational perception of the situation.

For example, my own core beliefs, etched in stone, tend to centre around feelings of failure and imperfection: 'I am not good enough' – not as good as other people at certain key things that I value in others: being fun, popular, competent, creative ... being – if I'm totally honest, although I probably would never admit this out loud – the 'best' at everything.

Without blinking, with my 'I'm not good enough' glasses on I seek evidence that I haven't achieved something as well as I could and therefore that I'm 'not very good', or that people don't like me very much, and this reiterates my core belief and perpetuates a negative cycle of self-sabotage. When applied to motherhood, with the heady mixture of exhaustion, insecurity, emotions and general discombobulation that lies there, if I'm not careful my core beliefs can steer my mental wellbeing onto a negative course.

Our automatic thoughts echo our core beliefs

The more unhelpful our core beliefs are, the more negative our automatic thoughts will be. So if I tuned in to my daily internal dialogue on a day where I'm feeling tired and low, I would notice it wittering on about how it's obvious I'm not very popular as my mum friends wandered off after school drop-off for a coffee together without inviting me, or that I don't have many likes on Instagram. I will forage around for *evidence* to back up these negative thoughts, which will add fuel to the core belief that I'm not as good as other people.

You are your own worst enemy if you listen to yourself without questioning the facts, and allow worst-case scenarios to present themselves as plausible situations. Your core beliefs create the *assumptions* that you apply to your behaviour in your life: the rules you live your life by. Take my core belief: 'I am a failure.' The assumption that that leads to is quite black and white: 'If I don't do something perfectly (in order to negate my rubbish feelings), then this must mean "I am a failure".'

If I stop and quieten my negative internal chatter for a moment, and instead seek more balanced evidence about my popularity and competence, I would see the fact that I have a totally wonderful variety of friends who think I'm as awesome as I think they are, that I have achieved some very cool and interesting things in my personal and professional life, and that, objectively, I'm actually a pretty well-rounded and 'successful' person.

I can find just as much positive evidence as negative, *if I look for it*. In the example of the mums wandering off for a coffee party without me after school drop-off, which confirms my feeling that I'm not popular, I *overlook the fact* that I received lots of lovely texts and offers of help from concerned mum friends the other day when both my kids were sick. But my internal chit-chat doesn't think that those kinds of truths are useful to hone in on. Therefore, positive evidence is disregarded/overlooked and the negative worldview persists.

ACTIVITY

Troubleshooting unhelpful thoughts

Keep a **thought diary** to detect and challenge negative thought patterns.

- Whenever you have a negative thought, notice it and write it down in your notebook, or on your phone.

- Make a point of noticing and jotting down whenever you feel that a thought is a self-critical one.

- Notice repeated patterns of negative thoughts – and any themes that emerge.

- Write them *all* down, so you can see them clearly in black and white. The fact that it might be disturbing to see them written down should show you how powerful these are in your head.

- Ask yourself *why* you make these assumptions to live your life by, using the *'if it were true, then ...'* technique: 'if that were true, what would it mean?'

Below are some examples of recurrent automatic thoughts that you might note down in your diary.

- 'I'm crap at being a mum.'
- 'I'm making a complete mess of dealing with my son's tantrums.'
- 'I'm never going to get to grips with my daughter's behaviour.'
- 'I'm no good at balancing work and motherhood.'

Taken together, these examples of a recurrent pattern of thought begin to unlock the core belief that you're incompetent: '*if* I don't do this perfectly, *then* I'm incompetent.'

This leads to an *assumption* that you must do everything you can do to complete tasks perfectly, and if you miss the bar even slightly, it will lead to feelings of distress and failure.

Take the following steps to bust your negative thought patterns.

1. Have a look at the recurrent themes and see if noticing them allows you to unlock what your core beliefs are – those that are informing your thought processes and day-to-day feelings. You may be surprised with what you uncover.

2. Start viewing yourself with a bit more kindness. I always think, if I would never be mean to my best friend, why do I feel it's OK to be mean to myself? Consider whether you're just being mean to yourself, every day, and commit to overturning this.

Other unhelpful thought patterns you may notice

All or nothing thinking: no shades of grey here – your brain will offer only extremes: 'If I can't deal with my toddler's tantrums I'm just never going to go outside in public'; 'I let them watch TV all afternoon today, therefore I'm a terrible mother.'

Mind reading/fortune telling: 'I know that the other mums don't like me'; 'I know it'll all go wrong if I try to do this.'

'Shoulds' and 'musts': 'I should be much better at doing crafts every day, otherwise I'm crap'; 'I must make the right decision, otherwise it'll be a disaster.'

Putting on your specs

Imagine your core beliefs are like glasses that colour how you view yourself, others and the world. Try out the following exercise and consider the questions.

1. If yours are an 'unlovable' pair of glasses, choose a colour and a style for them.

   Mentally visualise yourself putting them on and see what they do to your view of the world. Imagine yourself walking through the day with them on and see how they colour the way you see things.

   - How do they affect how you see your relationships with your friends, family, partner and children?
   - How do they change how you see yourself? Your life? Your work?

2. Now imagine taking them off.

   - How does the world look without them?

3. Try on another pair, e.g. an 'I am lovable' pair.

   - How would wearing these change how you think, feel, and respond to difficulties?

Extension: If it helps, you can actually buy a pair of glasses and do this exercise in real time.

Most of us don't know we wear these glasses, let alone that we *have the choice* to take them off or change them.

Mud sticks

Core beliefs are fairly unshakeable. They're rather like those annoying burrs that stick to your clothing like Velcro and take forever to unpick. Any evidence that disputes them tends to be ignored by your brain in a hands-in-ears 'la la la la I'm not listening' way, or simply viewed as the irrelevant exception to the rule: 'Yes, perhaps I *did* get a promotion straight after I came back from maternity leave, and I'm apparently well respected by all of my colleagues, but they don't really know the truth – that actually I am slightly rubbish and I make silly mistakes.'

Your core belief will always triumph unless it's faced with irrefutable evidence – such as that of Father Christmas being a made-up parental ruse for guaranteeing good behaviour in children – showing that you simply cannot continue to believe it once all facts mount up against it.

Be aware that your innermost, deepest beliefs will always try to *suggest* that they *are* true fact, and they're not going anywhere, thank you very much. We can get stuck in a negative trap and make the same thinking errors over and over – but we don't see them as 'errors', they're just our thoughts; we don't make the connection between our thought patterns and how we end up *feeling*: crap, lonely, angry, upset, empty. The more we make these errors, the more we *believe our negative thoughts* – and the harder it becomes to challenge them and see things in a different way.

Have a go at nudging your core beliefs out of their throne and allowing a more benevolent, balanced belief to take a seat. Core beliefs are incredibly important to our sense of self, and therefore it is quite a scary thing to shine a spotlight on them and try to work out how you came to these conclusions about yourself and, shock horror, perhaps try to change them. Imagine that they're not etched in stone but are actually written in the only kind of marker you should ever give a toddler: a washable one.

Think of it as a spring clean – taking a broom to sweep out the negative patterns in your brain and establish better thought patterns. In the same way that you go to the gym to shape up your body, this is exercising your mind in order to bring your mental health into better shape; it will take the same amount of work, but it will be worth it. By doing this, you can gain a more balanced view of what is going on. *You are a good, kind, caring mum whose children adore you.* Look for evidence that backs this up occasionally.

Master criminal at work

The notion of 'imposter syndrome' can affect us all at some point. Imposter syndrome is a concept describing high-achieving individuals who are unable to truly recognise their accomplishments because they have a persistent fear of being exposed as a 'fraud'. The term was coined in 1978 by clinical psychologists Pauline Clance and Suzanne Imes. Despite objective evidence of competence, 'imposters' remain convinced that they're frauds and don't deserve their success.

Any proof of success is dismissed as luck, timing, or a result of *deceiving* others into thinking they're more intelligent and competent than they actually are. These are all examples of how core beliefs maintain themselves. You might notice this, too: if you challenge your beliefs, you will find them fighting back by minimising or dismissing the evidence that you are presenting them with.

Imposter syndrome is often to be seen in the workplace, but it can also be felt as a mum, when you think you're just winging it and that everyone else seems to actually have it sorted. Women are more likely to internalise mistakes and criticism and label it as failure, while men are more likely simply to attribute these things to external factors.

It feels completely alien to call yourself a mum, particularly in the early days – that first walk with the buggy feels like a total charade – but if unchecked this feeling can continue. Hearing yourself say, 'I have two children' seems surreal and a bit too grown up sometimes. You're just playing at it, right? So we battle along, picking up socks and making packed lunches, with a niggling feeling that we're not good enough and are putting on a show of competence next to the mums who actually know what they're doing. But – think to yourself. If your mask is that good, then what are the odds that everyone else is also wearing a mask, some days?

We can't all be 'master criminals' – what in your mind does a truly authentic mum look like? Underlying this self-doubt is often a core belief like 'I am not good enough' – so if others knew the 'real' me, or knew what I was really like, they would see that I am actually not doing a good job at all of being a mum.

Alongside these beliefs come feelings of anxiety and fear of failing, and that leads us to behave in a way that keeps us safe from others finding this out – such as aiming for a show of perfection: this can manifest in a deep shame of your children's tantrums as they show you're not able to control your children; or staying up all night to make all of your children's Halloween costumes, Christmas cards and decorations from scratch so that you can prove you're a supermum at crafts. This then creates a cycle whereby you have to keep up this extra-high level of striving for perfection in fear of being exposed as a fraud ... basically, chasing your tail forever.

I was talking to a mum of two, Rosie, who is high up in a media company and works four days a week. She has recently split from her children's dad and is learning to live as a single mum while juggling her workload and the brilliant challenges that two- and four-year-old boys bring. So, all in all, she's got a hell of a lot going on. When I asked her how life was, she said, 'I'm being really crap at work at the moment, really bad. I feel I'm not on top of things at all.' It was clear to me that Rosie was acing it on so many levels, but she was focusing only on where she felt she was falling down most. And her benchmark for 'being crap' was probably very different from that of most of her colleagues.

Go and cause chaos – testing out your fears

ACTIVITY

There are a number of activities that psychologists often co-create with clients, essentially to test out the frightening thoughts they have. Here is one way of doing this, with a few alternative options for how to carry out the activity.

What is your biggest source of day-to-day anxiety? Write it down. Some common examples are that:

- your child will cause chaos by having a tantrum in the supermarket and everyone will think you are a failure

- you'll make a few silly mistakes, or one big mistake, at work because you're sleep deprived, and everyone at work will judge you as incompetent.

Then build an experiment to purposefully test out the fear you have identified. You can do this in one of the following ways.

1. **Create a survey** that asks a question such as: 'If you saw a mum and her child and the child did this, this, this – what would be your first thought?' Send it out to a group made up of people that you don't know so that you don't feel there is an inherent bias to their response – maybe a good place to use would be a Mumsnet forum or similar.

2. Or be brave and **ask a group of colleagues** if they feel they make small mistakes at work. Question them about:

- what they would think of as a small mistake and how regularly they think they make such mistakes

- how it makes them feel and what they think making small mistakes says about them as people

- how *they* would feel if they made a really big mistake – what would they think of themselves then?

It is interesting to have these discussions in order to explore the possibility that we are not thinking in the same way as others. It is useful also to weigh up how you would judge others' mistakes. We are often more generous towards other people.

3. **Mock up your scenario** to test your fear. The following is an example in which your anxieties are based around public meltdowns of your child.

- Don't avoid situations that cause you fear (e.g. a supermarket trip), but go into them.

- When the meltdown actually happens, take a moment to stop and breathe – and *notice* whether anyone is actually paying much attention at all.

- Letting go of the control can make you realise that it's *not the end of the world.* You may actually see either that people totally ignore you or that they are offering you the silent mum nod of empathy.

- Pausing to notice, and breathe, may also simply help to diffuse the situation and make you realise that, inherently, people do not pay as much attention to us as we think they do.

Our worst fears in these situations are unlikely to ever be as bad as we imagine, simply because other people do not have the spotlight on us in the way that we do. Realising that other people view your situation differently/with less emotion can allow you to reframe it for yourself.

Remember, if we had worried about falling over when we were babies we would never have learnt to walk.

Learning to reframe your thoughts about failure and competence is absolutely vital for shooing away your supermum imposter and allowing your real, perfectly good mum self to sit down and have a cup of tea in peace.

Helicopter

In clinical psychology, there is a term called 'helicoptering', which is the skill of being able to step outside of a situation and try to look at it objectively.

The next time you are in a stressful situation, silently try helicoptering above it.

- Imagine yourself flying (maybe even inside a helicopter) over your situation. If you were looking down, what would you think?
- Notice what fresh insights you have.
- Notice what you think about this mum, and your emotional response to her.

Your supermum imposter voice responds to a complicated scenario, such as the first trip out with a new baby and a toddler, with: 'Oh my god, I have no idea what I'm doing, this is hell on wheels, everyone will think I'm a total failure.' Real, perfectly good mum self, with her peaceful cup of tea, will think: 'Wow, OK, so this is going to be chaos and possibly carnage, but I'm going to learn a lot and it will get easier over time, and those looks in the playground are sympathy looks, not looks of horror at my incompetence.'

*'I listen to mums with two or more kids talk about their days and what they're juggling and what they struggle with, and I think …
I only have one and I'm a total shambles, I don't have any right to find this so difficult as I only have one, what on earth would I be like with two?'*

Sarah, mum of one

Non-imposters (the real, perfectly good mums) realise that everyone has the right to have good days and bad, and that some things just come more easily than others. Know that the same things happen; they just don't see them (they don't have the same cognitive bias) or interpret them in the same way. Your unique mum skill might be whipping up a brilliant last-minute costume out of toilet paper and socks for World Book Day, but you're rubbish at maths homework. Someone else will be crap at costumes but a winner at making cheese muffins. You win some, you lose some – this is life.

Your immediate response to seeing an example of 'stronger mum game' than yours is that they are brilliant, and you're obviously therefore rubbish. Well if they're brilliant at something that you don't excel in, honestly, so what? You can't be brilliant at everything. But you *are* brilliant at lots of things and are just not seeing it. Focus on the things that you do, and not the things that you don't.

Getting out of your head

If you feel that sometimes your internal dialogue gets the better of you and it becomes like a negative loop, it's always useful to connect to your body and try to release your mind from its overworking.

ACTIVITY

Press pause – connect to your body

If your mind goes into overdrive, give yourself a time limit for worrying.

Sit down with your notebook, and for 15 minutes write down and focus on exactly what it is that is troubling you.

Or, take those 15 minutes to worry while you're doing something productive, like the washing up, making tea or brushing your teeth.

After 15 minutes/the action is finished, let it go. Stop. Change your focus to something else.

Try the following actions.

- **Mindful awareness of your body.** Lie down. Scan your body from the toes up, breathing deeply, for at least 15 minutes. Focus purely on your in-breath and your out-breath, nothing more. Allow thoughts to wander past like clouds across the sky, but don't invite them to linger.

- **Move.** Getting your energy flowing will change the energy in your mind. Marching or jogging on the spot, dancing, maybe with your children (or, better, alone if they're anything like mine – 'STOP DANCING MUMMY!').

- **Do some yoga or go swimming; get into a physical 'flow'**, which will shift your mental perception and release endorphins.

- **Listen to music**, or your favourite podcast.
- **Stop yourself reasoning** or explaining to yourself within your head. If you are having a debate, an argument, analysing things too much *to yourself*, pause and realise there is simply no need. Just be.

3

Birthing supermum: your pregnancy, birth and beyond

This chapter takes you through where your perfect motherhood vision stems from, and how our mama characteristics are informed and shaped by our experiences of fertility and birth.

More than in any other chapter of your mothering story, pregnancy, birth and the first year of being a mum is where you're confronted with your imagined ideal locking horns with your reality. Imagined: dreamy water birth, listening to Buddhist chanting while husband lovingly strokes your glowing forehead as you breathe calmly through your contractions. Reality: mooing like a cow on your hands and knees, cursing like a sailor and demanding that you want an epidural, while holding your partner in a headlock.

It's this disparity between expectation and reality that enables the feelings of failure to creep in, and your supermum vision to shatter around you before it's even begun.

'Before I had children, I assumed that it was hard work but if you just put the effort in then it was OK. I thought unhappy or unruly

kids were the result of a "lack of planning" on behalf of the parents.'

Debbie, mum of two

With your perfect supermum picture in place before you even have your baby, you're nicely set up for feeling inadequate and incompetent if motherhood demands leave you feeling that you don't live up to your own, and society's, expectations of 'normal'.

Great expectations

What was your vision of motherhood before you had a baby? When I was pregnant with my first, I had a drawer that I lovingly filled with baby paraphernalia: Babygros, tiny socks, cosy sleeping bags invoking images of a content, sleeping baby. I thought having a baby might be like having a cat: they were loving, cuddly, but somehow also independent – you'd be able to go to the loo or make toast without constantly holding them. There'd be tiredness, but you've been tired before and it can't be much worse than how you feel after an all-night party or working late, can it ...? Maternity leave would be a holiday, a time to sort out the house, to write that novel ...

Nearly all of the mums I interviewed for this book admitted to having felt a huge sense of shock at how bloody hard it was at the start, and a feeling of 'why doesn't anyone *tell* you this?!' The great motherhood conspiracy: better not tell anyone in case they don't want to do it as a result. As much as you can't really describe adequately how hard being a mum is, you also can't effectively describe how much greater the rewards are than for any other job you would ever do.

> *'I remember feeling furious with every mother I knew who didn't tell me, warn me, that motherhood was an awful, awful thing to do – I felt tricked by evolution and society and convinced I would never be, and was not worthy of being, a good mother.'*
>
> Amy, mum of two

Your fertility journey

Self-flagellation tendencies can begin even before you become pregnant. It's possible to class yourself a failure or feel an underlying sense of shame because you haven't been able to conceive naturally, when everyone around you seems to get pregnant by just sniffing their partner's aftershave. Or if, like me, you didn't have much trouble *getting* pregnant, but *staying* pregnant became a bit of a drama with several miscarriages – why am I so rubbish at keeping a single foetus alive when there are programmes on TV about one woman having 19 children?

This taps into our core-belief system once more. Rather than taking it at face value, for example that I was sadly and simply having a problem on my fertility road, as many of us do, I – without realising it at the time – attributed it to my inherent failure to do things as well as other people, and used it as a tiny mallet to hit myself around the head with.

Fertility problems are sadly still a bit of a taboo subject, and maybe not something you'd chat about lightheartedly on the bus. There is relentless societal pressure on women not to 'leave it too late' to have children. The selfish act of refusing to have a child at the right time is for some weird reason laid solely at the feet of the woman, when in actual fact it's a complicated life game of dominoes that have to be lined up, and they don't always fall the way society would like them to. A lengthy, prolonged and uncertain fertility journey can adversely affect your mental state during pregnancy and well into motherhood if you don't ever give yourself a chance to let it go.

> '*I didn't realise at the time, but something had been taken away from me and I couldn't get it back – the chance to have a baby naturally. So this was a heartbreaking time for me and my husband. I slowly acknowledged the loss to myself and realised it was a kind of bereavement. I felt like I wasn't a "proper woman", and a feeling of embarrassment kicked in.'*
>
> Mina, mum of two IVF girls

If you're reading this book, then you have presumably reached your ultimate destination of being able to have a child, by whichever means you had to get there. You may not even have taken the time to explore any unresolved feelings about the difficulties you've had along the way, and how these might be affecting your wellbeing and allowing you a sense of imperfection in your mum role now.

Visualising your fertility journey

Think about the road that you travelled along in order to reach your child/children. Visualise your journey as a physical walk through a landscape.

Was it a straightforward walk around a picturesque reservoir? Or was it at points more of a mountain trek?

1. Take some time to think about how this journey has made you the mum you are. Map out the visuals as an actual journey (both the lighter and tougher elements). Write it down, or even draw it, if this helps you to explore it and bring it to life.

2. Ask yourself questions about your journey.

   - What qualities did you discover in your rucksack that helped you along the way?

   - Who else accompanied you on all/aspects of it?

   - What talents and resources did you find along the way that helped you get through?

3. Finally, ask yourself about how you felt and what you had learnt when you reached your destination.

   - What aspects of that journey were you glad to leave at the end?

   - What was valuable to take with you into the next journey stage of motherhood?

Case study: An IVF experience

Juliet was 34 when she and her husband decided it was the right time to think about having a new small person in their house.

'I just assumed having a baby would be the next thing on the list, particularly as we put off trying so we would be married first. I just thought you got married, tick, then got pregnant, tick. You spend your adult life taking every precaution in the world to avoid getting pregnant as if it would ruin your life, so you imagine once you stop taking those precautions, it'll just happen. After a year of trying, we both thought something couldn't be right as everyone else seemed to be pregnant who had got married after us … maybe that wasn't important, but all I could focus on was being "overtaken" by other couples.'

They were eventually diagnosed with 'unexplained fertility'. Juliet says, 'the diagnosis was so unhelpful because it meant neither of us could do anything or even usefully blame ourselves, yet of course we both did ... Or I certainly did anyway.' They qualified for three free rounds of IVF on the NHS and were lucky that there wasn't a long waiting list in their area. Juliet was a career girl with a high-energy, long-hours, high-stress job in PR. They approached the first round of IVF with optimism and excitement. 'When it didn't work, it was absolutely crushing because I had really expected it to, I naïvely hadn't really allowed myself to consider the alternative.'

Juliet didn't allow herself a break in terms of rebalancing her body after all the fertility drugs, or rebooting her mind after the hormonal surges and emotional overload, and was continuing with her working and social life at full speed as always. They embarked on their second round. Still no luck. They went for their third.

'At this point we barely had a relationship ... we didn't prioritise "us" any more, it was all about the IVF, all roads led back to it. But we hadn't really told many people so we were kind of trapped in it. My 36th birthday came and went, and suddenly everyone seemed to have an opinion about me having a baby, it felt like. Constant remarks about not putting off having children, and questions about plans for babies. I was even called a "selfish career woman" jokily by someone at work ... I just wanted to scream at him that I hadn't gone out of my way to leave it too late to have a baby, it just wasn't happening for me.'

Their free IVF rounds used up, they faced a choice about how much more they wanted to financially invest, after a gruelling emotional and physical investment up until now. They decided to gather together all of their savings, and see whether they could go for another push.

After a failed round four, Juliet threw herself fully into working and partying. She wasn't really conscious of it at the time but her family and friends were concerned that she was suppressing her feelings of loss and failure by self-medicating with booze and nights out, withdrawing from her husband by regularly staying out until the early hours. 'It seems really obvious looking back, but I just stopped engaging with Rob at home and wanted to blot everything out, drink all night until 3a.m. as if I was a student again, while also keeping it together at work. I was slightly falling apart, I can see that now, but I didn't have anyone I felt I could talk to about it all and I was just so sick of it not working, and bitter that I couldn't do what everyone else I knew could do so easily.'

They got through the dark period – 'I don't really know how we didn't split up' – and they decided to pour the last of their money into a final last chance fifth round of IVF. Success at last, and Juliet had a baby girl. But her pregnancy wasn't free from stress: she had bleeding and thought she might lose the baby. 'I had such awful mixed emotions, thinking, I can't lose this baby as I might never have another chance – I was already imagining having to go through IVF again and again, after losing this baby.'

When she was in her third trimester her husband had a skiing accident, which put him in intensive care for weeks. 'I couldn't help but just think, how is this happening?! He's stealing my chance to "glow" in the late part of my pregnancy, and then I hated myself for having these thoughts … I felt like the whole pregnancy experience of joy that you see everywhere was completely denied to me.'

Making sense of a traumatic fertility experience

ACTIVITY

What Juliet experienced is a mass of repeated loss, trauma and stress, which she has assimilated and added to her backpack of core beliefs and assumptions about herself. She just packed it all away and got on with the day-to-day business of being a mum, possibly without noticing how it has impacted upon her daily automatic thoughts, negative internal dialogue or heightened feelings of anxiety.

- Imagine a filing cabinet.
- Even draw a filing cabinet, with different compartments, in your notebook.
- You could label each compartment: 'fear', 'shame', 'anxiety', 'sadness', 'anger', etc.
- Write down your thoughts and feelings about your fertility journey, the types of details that Juliet has uncovered here, details that you may feel are inconsequential.
- Rummage through exactly what may be making you feel fearful/shameful/anxious/sad/angry about your experience.
- Give it a clear voice through writing it down, acknowledging it, and then file it away in an appropriate file.

Day to day, often we cope with an experience such as this in all sorts of ways, without addressing it head-on until we have a time when we can rummage through it and work it out.

Acknowledge that *you did your best* under the circumstances.

Adoption – if I wasn't pregnant, am I a 'real' mother?

Anna, an adoptive mum of two school-age children, says, 'I sometimes feel like I can't really pitch in to conversations about motherhood with other school mums when they talk about their kids when they were in their tummies, or even simple things like when they're annoyed that others comment that their children only look like their dads and not them ... if I do ever chip in I feel like they must think I'm a bit of a fraud who doesn't have a right to an opinion.' If adoption has come from your trying to conceive naturally and being unable to, your own emotional needs are particularly important, but too often overlooked.

Then add this to the baby's or child's needs, which always take priority, and it can become a complicated tapestry of self-care being placed on the backburner and never quite figuring out how you can find an equilibrium with these feelings. You may feel that as you've missed 'the start' you're constantly trying to catch up to prove your legitimate worth as a mum. Your child might have come to you some time after birth – Anna adopted her children at ages five and seven – so they were 'fully formed people I had to get to know and grow into being their mum.'

You may get limited information about their biological family and any potential issues, which can be the cause of some anxiety spiralling about what might lie ahead. You might have an expectation also that you are going to 'fix this little one' or make up for their start in life, if they've had a difficult beginning. So you have to be mindful of setting yourself an impossible scenario in which you want to be Supermum to prove to yourself you are a 'real mum', while also simply wanting to be an amazing mum to give your child the best life you can.

Vanessa has two children. She carried them both, but after lengthy fertility struggles she had eventually become pregnant with donor eggs. 'I constantly worry about when we should tell them that they're not really my children ... that they're actually from another mum – I just happened to carry them in my belly and give birth to them. It worries me what that will do to them and whether they'll just stop loving me.'

From an objective point of view, it is clear that these mothers are *obviously* parents. It is particularly heartbreaking that the mum who gave birth to donor-egg babes is so dismissive of her intrinsically mothering role of carrying her babies in her womb for nine months, and working hard to transport them earthside safely.

These are all bricks carefully placed in the great wall of love that is built over time. So it's all about the thinking – if they aren't yours, well, whose are they? Find terminology that works for you and allows you to acknowledge the dominant role you have – for example, the 'egg' parent, 'biological' and 'birth' parents have a small role. *You* are their mum.

Mind the bump

Your mental health during pregnancy can have a huge impact on the way that you tackle the first crucial months of motherhood and attachment forming. If you struggled with fertility issues or miscarriage, you may well have experienced antenatal anxiety during your pregnancy. We all hear about postnatal depression, but perhaps not enough about perinatal: symptoms of low mood, anxiety and trauma, which can start during pregnancy and then continue beyond.

It may be that you experienced it without having realised or acknowledged it to yourself, and were therefore more susceptible to these feelings being exacerbated in the fog of exhaustion after your baby was born. Having talked to so many mums about this in researching this book, it's clear that it's often only in hindsight that you're aware of quite how low you were feeling and so it didn't even occur to you to find strategies to deal with it.

You may have sailed through your first pregnancy in a rosy glow, but second time round had a totally different perception and saw your pre-baby self as naïve, not understanding the full force of the typhoon heading her way. Second pregnancies can be veiled with a predominantly negative feeling, even, because of having more idea of what was to come if you found it a horror show first time round.

'When I got pregnant with my second, all I could think was that we were going to have to go back to the dark days again.'
Polly, mum of two

I met a best friend for coffee and she announced to me that she was pregnant with her second; her first baby was just over a year old. She pushed a scan picture towards me over the table with a sigh ... and said, faux brightly, 'yeah ... so I know that I've got at least another ten weeks of puking and feeling awful ahead of me, and another two years at least of not sleeping at all ... great!' I felt really troubled by how low she seemed at the time, but after I had had a baby of my own I entirely understood why she had that mixed sense of happy resignation rather than total jubilation.

There is no societal warm hug for feelings like this attached to pregnancy – it's supposed to be an unambiguously blissful time, which means it's easy to berate yourself for not feeling like you enjoyed it, or made the most of it, or glowed enough.

Comparison is the thief of joy, said Theodore Roosevelt. This is a recurring refrain in our quest to debunk the supermum myth: you're bobbing along fine until something triggers you to compare yourself to someone else who you feel is doing it better than you, and suddenly you are filled with feelings that you're a bit crap.

With pregnancy, particularly if you succumb to negative mental thought patterns with anxiety and low mood, there are so many ways to feel like you didn't reach the heady heights that you could have: in your pregnancy body, style, health and mood.

When I was pregnant, if anyone close to me mentioned in passing how another pregnant woman was looking 'amazing', or 'fantastic', the lack of a similar comment directed at me ensured I took it to mean that I was looking like a bloated Michelin Man, that I wasn't somehow doing pregnancy justice by looking great. Notice whether your feeling of 'underachieving' in motherhood begins with your mindset about your pregnancy experience. And if it does, see if you can find ways to break that down and begin to see your mothering from a more positive perspective.

Birth

Childbirth is considered to be a natural, joyful event. So no wonder we feel like we've failed at the first hurdle of reaching supermum heights if we can't actually get that initial bit 'right'. Your first birth experience and its immediate aftermath frames your mood and sets the tone of your experience of early motherhood and beyond. You might bring your feelings from this birth into the way that you approach motherhood, and into subsequent birth experiences. It doesn't have to have been a textbook 'horror story' to have shocked you to your very core.

We have a real 'carrying-on-as-normal' set-up soon after birth in our society, for example in birthing units where it is expected that you can get up and leave after six hours. While acknowledging birth *is* a natural and normal process, this can also lead to first-time mums having the expectation that the 'gold standard' of birthing is that you should be up and about, preferably in your skinny jeans, within hours of experiencing one of the most intense and difficult physical experiences you will probably ever have to go through.

> 'My second birth was really swift, everything went well ... I shouldn't have anything to complain about, but it really left me in a state of shock. I felt like I'd been in an accident, like I was emerging from a wreckage or something ... maybe it was too fast, I don't know.'
>
> Natalie, mum of two

> 'I feel like my birth experience was so horrific that it absolutely has meant that I don't ever want to have any more children. I had no control, I was terrified, it lasted longer than anyone else's labour I know of, it was more painful than I could have ever imagined. I never, ever, want to go through anything like that again.'
>
> Lucie, mum of one

Often we see the birth as the endgame – almost like a World Cup Final, we focus on that one event that we need to 'win' and get stickers or a medal for. Instead surely we should look at it as a gateway to motherhood to get through, climb over, however we need to in order to get to the other side for high fives all round. There can be pressure from yourself, your family and society for a 'perfect birth'. Pressure to wholeheartedly love and adore your baby from the moment it is born. And if you fall short of this 'perfection' at the starting blocks, that feeling can linger with you throughout the whole event.

Clemmie Hooper, midwife and author of How to Grow a Baby and Push it Out, was one of the community midwives I was lucky enough to have caring for me during my second pregnancy. She once said that everyone focuses on the birth rather than looking towards the job of motherhood – but there is no epidural for motherhood.

My own birthing expectations versus reality

First time round, being a bit of a hippy at heart, I was completely sure I was going to have a calm, hypnobirthing natural birth. I read all the books, I did all the meditation, I did hours and hours of yoga, beckoning my baby peacefully earthside with images of opening lilies and surging waves. I knew that I wasn't going to have an epidural as that would be 'bad': I would try to be in water, I would be upright and mobile throughout, I would be positive, confident and empowered to tell midwives what I wanted in the moment.

Cut to nearly 42 weeks pregnant. I was induced, fell meekly to the authority of anyone in a white coat rather than trusting my instincts at all, and had the full gamut of intervention thrown at me, ultimately begging for an epidural after two days of labouring without pain relief. Long story short, I ended up with a category 1 emergency caesarean – a crash caesarean as my baby's life was at stake.

Nothing in my mental preparation had imagined my birthing room being suddenly rushed by medical staff with such a sense of urgency, being sped down a corridor on a trolley so that you can be prepped for surgery and have your baby pulled out within 15 minutes of the call being made. He wasn't breathing when he was born, and the following minutes of waiting to see how the dice rolled remain pretty much the worst of my life.

In the months after his birth, I kept repeating to myself, with my unquestioned automatic thoughts, that my body had let me down, that I hadn't prepared in the right way. That I had failed. A close family friend had been due at the same time as me, and she had had a smooth home birth four days earlier, where they had been eating pizza blissfully in bed with their newborn within hours of giving birth.

It felt (to my unquestioned thoughts) like everyone around me was celebrating how brilliantly she had done, commenting on how amazing she looked, and giving me critical 'better luck next time, never mind that you were a bit crap' vibes in comparison. Even the terminology that you find in your birthing notes is heavily laced with judgemental vocabulary: 'failure to progress', 'incompetent cervix'.

It can be bittersweet looking at my eldest, knowing that bringing him into the world isn't filled with memories of joy and sweaty euphoria, but instead fear, pain, shock, being utterly out of control and powerless. I felt like I failed *him* by not being able to birth him naturally, with all the guilt bombarded upon you about the benefits for your baby of a natural birth. And I now feel sad that I can't lovingly relay to him what a wonderful day we had when Mummy bounced on a birthing ball happily, listening to Beyoncé and eating Hobnobs, and then popped you out blissfully on the living-room floor.

I've spoken to many women while compiling stories for this book, and my birth experience is echoed a thousand times by others having been through similar. The words 'train wreck', 'car crash', 'nightmare' and 'horrific' kept coming up, the common thread being that every single one of us seemed to label ourselves a failure and feel guilty because of one or all aspects of what we felt we did 'wrong'. We compound this feeling and carry it around like a rucksack full of rocks for years without even considering it's there. Listen to how you talk about your own birth experience. It will be triggering a whole emotional response deep in your gut that you're not even aware of.

If you've had a difficult birth experience you can be left thinking, 'I wish I'd done this instead', and this can lead to ruminating over the same parts of the birth that you are unhappy with. 'I wish I'd said this ...', 'I could have done more', 'I could have tried harder.' Underneath these thoughts can be the core belief 'I'm weak.' It can be helpful to think about the birth in a different way. Were there times during the birth when you showed strength, no matter how small? Some women describe trying to move or speak (even if they couldn't due to medication) or trying to control their own minds – by taking it out of the situation, shifting their focus or telling themselves, 'It'll be over soon.'

An army of warrior mothers

When I was on the operating table after having my first, I was told that I'd had a boy, but that he wasn't breathing. In the eerie yet busy silence while they set about resuscitating him – no hearty newborn cries to be heard – I remember feeling like a truck was sitting on my chest and I couldn't breathe. I later understood that this was most likely to be the effects of the anaesthetic reaching too high into my chest, but I didn't logically know that at the time. I decided to coax myself away from what I thought was a rising panic attack by focusing on calmly counting to ten, then back to one, then up to ten, over and over again.

I now hold on to that as a sign that I didn't actually break in that moment, despite being put under immense pressure. On closer analysis, maybe there were things you did that showed real strength, and that importantly there were good reasons why you could not do more of what you wanted to.

Emma, a mum of two, went through not one but two traumatic birth experiences. 'My second labour had a huge impact as I simply wasn't present for the first 16 weeks of my daughter's life; I don't remember the magic, I don't remember my son learning to be a big brother, loving his sister. In those weeks I simply fed her when needed and handed her to someone else as I hurt so much. I was taking all painkillers available to me and was still in pain most of the time, not sleeping, and struggling to breastfeed a tongue-tied baby. I was determined to breastfeed both of my babies because of my feelings of failure around their births; I couldn't fail at that too.'

The immense pressure we put on ourselves to get birth 'right' takes its toll on our mental health. Emma felt like she wasn't present, she was 'merely existing' for the first four months of her daughter's life. She was eventually diagnosed as having post-traumatic stress disorder (PTSD, see page 75).

Sometimes it's not so much the birth but the aftermath that can leave you suffering trauma. Vicky, a mum of one, says, 'I actually quite enjoyed giving birth, everything went really well. It was after that it all came crashing down around my ears. My son was very ill and was taken away immediately to the NICU, and ultimately had to have heart surgery when he was only hours old.'

Going through your notes with a midwife (at the right time for you) can help in seeing the bigger picture and helping you to piece together the jigsaw of the birth. Feel empowered by the fact that there is a whole army of us warrior women who have experienced a powerful and difficult birth experience but who have got out the other side.

Body shock

Breastfeeding – the most natural and yet most challenging thing you will ever have to learn how to do and one of the most popular areas for mums to label themselves a 'failure'. Yes, some mums take to it like Lady Madonna, but most women struggle and are simply shocked by how bloody hard and painful it is. Or are uncomfortable with how trapped it makes them feel. Or feel judged for not wanting to do it at all. Or try to do a combination of breast and bottle and still can't find the inner peace. There are no winners, it seems, if you are aiming to achieve supermum status with an 'I won at breastfeeding!' sticker.

'My milk didn't come in, despite routine expressing and – when my baby was finally out of NICU – breastfeeding. I felt a complete failure. How could I not fulfil this most basic part of mothering, nourishing your child? I was constantly in tears and felt under pressure to express and feed and supplement, a routine that took an hour and had to take place every three hours and be completely documented. It drove me crazy. And still after a week, I was only producing 5ml of colostrum every time I expressed. I had imagined days of skin-to-skin contact and feeding, but was not allowed to sleep in the same room as my son for the first two days and then he was in an incubator for another day. I felt like a failure before I had really started.'

Elizabeth, mum of two

Warrior mum

In your notebook, or on your computer, at a time that feels safe and right for you, write down your birth story and whatever about your birthing experience that leaves you with feelings of failure.

If you are suffering from PTSD (see page 75), be mindful that re-enacting may be a trigger, and make sure that you feel comfortable exploring events.

- Every time you reach a part of the story that you feel represents an area where you failed, say out loud to yourself, and write down, 'I am a warrior.'

- Turn around your feelings of failure to represent feelings of supreme strength in adversity, where actually you coped well when things sped off course.

- Notice every time you think the word 'failed' about yourself and actively turn it around to 'triumphed'.

Memory-box ritual

It helps us to focus our thoughts and conjure up positive memories if we can create rituals. This is a ritual to allow you to bring together a collection of good things relating to your birth experience, and keep them all in one place.

- If you can, get hold of a memory trinket box, preferably not just a shoebox but one that you love the look of and would like to keep forever.

- Take some time to find and gather some mementoes of your birth experience: your baby's wrist or ankle label from the hospital, a photo, a hair band, a CD.

- Hold and touch each memento: close your eyes and notice how it makes you feel; accept that feeling without trying to interpret or change it.

- Write yourself a card congratulating yourself on the birth of your baby, and add this to the box.

- Close the box, and see this as a way of enclosing and acknowledging your negative associations with your birth.

There are two halves to this activity – one of *noticing the emotions* (in all their depth) and the other of *reminding yourself about what you achieved.*

Closing the box is not necessarily about letting go of the experience – but it is 'enclosing it', putting it away to give yourself a space away from it.

You can get it out again as you need to. This may be an activity to repeat at various points.

PND ... that's not me ... is it?

Was it depression, or just body-slamming fatigue? Was my baby's bad birth all my fault? We all hear a lot about PND – postnatal depression – and I don't know about you, but I expected it, if it arrived, to hit as a clear black fog and be 'obviously' depression. But, sadly, it doesn't work like that, so a lot of us can be feeling like we're desperately rowing a small boat in choppy seas for months, years, not attributing any of our feelings to depression as we don't think it's 'as serious as that'.

PND is on a spectrum, and a high level of anxiety and low mood is to be expected within this context. Recent research shows that symptoms of PND can even peak *four years* after the birth of your baby – it's not as clear cut as you might think, that it 'arrives' when your baby is a newborn. So we just keep rowing in our small boat to get through until the storm passes.

> 'Before I had children, I thought I would take it in my stride (as I did with life generally) and that I'd enjoy it. But I really didn't. Becoming a mum – the birth, the early days – it was all a massive shock to the system and I didn't cope very well at all.'
>
> Hannah, mum of two

PND is not all about you – there's a complicated mix of external risk factors beyond your control, which include traumatic birth, previous loss, your own early childhood experiences, lack of support, illness and the temperament of your baby. I personally didn't identify with the label 'postnatal depression' because of its implications of not bonding with your baby, not being able to ever laugh and engage happily in the moment. Remember also that experiencing low feelings is a *normal* response to the circumstances. My newborn cried constantly and didn't sleep for longer than an hour at a time overnight for months. It would, frankly, have been weird if I'd been feeling joyous.

Kelly, a mum of two, feels similarly. She says, 'I think the black and whiteness of "you either get postnatal depression or you don't" is massively misleading. I still have no idea if it's normal to cry as much as I did in those early days (and I mean far beyond the three-day baby blues blip, which frankly sounds tame compared to how I felt!).

'I also felt completely unprepared for the huge anxiety I would feel about my baby's health, and that the often well-meaning but matronly comments from health visitors and doctors would leave me in a complete tizz, unable to decipher what it meant, what I should do (keep breastfeeding or not? "You are her mother," they would say, "only you can decide"), and how to cope with all that uncertainty. It is hard to separate out what was exhaustion, hormones or proper depression. I still have no idea if I had postnatal depression after my first; I know I cried at least once every day and felt completely overwhelmed, but I did not live through the stereotypical behaviour changes we are all warned to look out for: reclusiveness, inability to bond, etc. I think postnatal depression is probably hugely underdiagnosed, and there are many shades of grey, and I would not be surprised if everyone doesn't suffer from it at least a little.'

'I was floored by my c-section, and I think I was too afraid to admit that motherhood was completely different from what I thought it was going to be. And [I felt] simply overwhelmed by the life-changing (physically, emotionally, socially) event of becoming a mum. I just needed to know that one day I WILL sleep again. That it was normal ... but on a daily basis I would silently be crying behind my sunglasses as I walked (my screaming baby) down the street, wondering why every mum I passed looked like they were coping brilliantly and I wasn't.'
Jade, mum of one

I personally felt an immense, overwhelming love for my baby, but on the flip side there was extreme exhaustion and shockingly debilitating pain from caesarean and breastfeeding (why doesn't anyone prepare new mums for how painful that is?!). And why, why will he not stop crying? I experienced heightened anxiety, unsettling worst-case scenario thoughts, and huge feelings of failure about my birth and breastfeeding struggles. I started to withdraw from meeting up with people or going anywhere on public transport as I didn't know how to deal with my constantly crying baby in public.

These are all on the PND spectrum – I realise this now – and, in retrospect, I should have sought help and support rather than battling on through simply wondering why I wasn't coping as well as others seemed to be. A diagnosis of PND can mean different things for different people, but *not* wanting one shouldn't get in the way of pulling some support in around you, however you can do this.

Case study: Postnatal depression

PND is something that is possibly more ubiquitous than we imagine, because it is still shrouded in taboo and fear of being honest about low feelings as a new mum. Like Sadie, who is a midwife and a mum of two, you can externally be functioning 'fine' and not appear to be struggling, but this belies what is going on behind the scenes.

'I was housebound due to recovering from a complicated c-section and I just didn't have the energy to go out much – although my mum and friends did visit and come and take me out but it felt like I was wading through treacle I was so tired. I struggled to find clothes to wear for breastfeeding initially and this was a transition for me as I usually liked different clothes and fashions. I knew I was coping in that I was going through the motions and I wanted to do everything for my baby boy but I just didn't "feel myself". I didn't really feel anything anymore – I "knew" my feelings in my head but didn't "feel" them.

'I also started to have irrational fears of things like nappy bags and ways my baby could be harmed; I knew that they were ridiculous but still kept having these intrusive thoughts. Eventually when Fred was about four weeks a card arrived that a friend had made. She had taken our birth pics off Facebook and put them on a picture collage card for us. It was so thoughtful and gorgeous and I looked at my happy self in those pictures and I knew I had to do something about the way I was feeling. I called the health visitor and told her I thought I had postnatal depression.

'The GP receptionist was helpful as I told her and she got an emergency appointment for that afternoon. Then I phoned my husband in work and told him. He wanted to come home immediately but I told him not to as I was going out for lunch with my friends! A few of my midwife colleagues had babies within short succession so we were going out to catch up. I dried my tears, did my hair, put on my make up and went out for lunch. No one would have known half an hour before what a mess I was in!

'As I sat there that lunchtime I heard the advice I was giving to my friends about how to cope with new motherhood; the irony was not lost on me that I couldn't seem to listen to or believe my own words. My husband collected me later that afternoon and the GP was really supportive. He suggested medication but told me I would have to stop breastfeeding, which was the end of the world to me at that point, so I told him I would do my research and talk to our obstetrician with mental health specialist interest and be in touch. The following day I spoke to the GP and got the medication I wanted to continue breastfeeding.

'Even just doing that made me feel better. I was taking action, and would get better, so I could cope with feeling so bad. My mum came round for a couple of weeks most days, to look after Fred in the day while I slept, and I was referred for CBT, which was really helpful. Within two months I felt more normal, and was off meds by the time he was five months old.'

'Healing' second births

If you had a shocking birth experience first time round, there is often huge pressure to 'heal' a bad first birth by doing it better the second time. To 'prove' yourself and do it 'right' ... but this can lead to even greater feelings of failure if it doesn't quite come off.

A very difficult 'natural' birth after a caesarean, for example, can lead to a physically bad recovery, as well as mental and emotional scars, which can leave you feeling worse off than you did the first time.

Emma had had a traumatic caesarean birth with her first, and therefore was determined to overturn this bad experience with a redemptive and blissful natural second birth. An even more traumatic VBAC (vaginal birth after caesarean) experience left her struggling physically, and she had to move back in with her mum in order to cope with the demands of her toddler while she healed and recovered her strength; she was eventually diagnosed as suffering from PTSD. She's not the only one I interviewed who had had a similar experience because of setting themselves the goal of 'perfect second birth'.

> 'Looking back, I nearly killed myself in the attempt to have a better birth experience second time round as I thought I had failed and was so angry about my caesarean. As a result I ended up haemorrhaging and in intensive care for four days because I was so determined not to have any intervention that it all went horribly wrong, and I wasn't able to even hold my second baby for two days. I ended up with PND and I'm sure it was due to beating myself up about doing it right. If I could do it again I would have had an elective section and been kinder to myself.'
>
> Louise, mum of two

Post-traumatic stress disorder (PTSD)

A traumatic birth may create an emotional environment in which you're more susceptible to PND. When a woman has found her birth experience very distressing, or even terrifying, it is possible that she can develop a related, but different, condition that is often misdiagnosed as PND: post-traumatic stress disorder. Symptoms include nightmares, excessive irritability, anxiety and flashbacks, leading to great distress, with any reminders of the event – smells, sounds, objects – acting as triggers.

Reconciling yourself to a horrific birth experience can be a complex process that may be different for everyone. It's worth remembering this quote from the poet Robert Frost: 'Don't take a fence down until you know why it has been put up.' There are often very good reasons why we defend against things, so making sure we feel *safe* enough before we go there, and that we are always in control of the process, is paramount.

> 'I was at the doctor's surgery trying to push for a diagnosis for PTSD after the birth of my second – I was sure that something wasn't right, and a friend who was a psychologist had said to me that she thought I was showing signs of it. My doctor

> *dismissed that it was PTSD I was suffering ... I left her office and went to the loo, and the soap dispenser was the same as the one I had had in my labour room, which triggered a flashback and a panic attack. My doctor quickly changed her diagnosis and referred me for counselling.'*
>
> Emma, mum of two

Some women find that writing it all in a journal helps to release it. Others might just want to talk and talk about their experience. Others, like Emma quoted above, actually want the opposite and prefer to withdraw completely. Whatever you have felt, if you're still experiencing what you suspect to be PTSD – even if your birth happened years ago – seek guidance, and don't allow your concerns to be dismissed as 'simply part of being a mum'. It doesn't have to be traumatic.

Trauma-focused CBT and Eye Movement Desensitisation and Reprocessing (EMDR) are currently recommended by the National Institute for Health and Care Excellence (NICE) as the best treatments for PTSD. Counselling may be helpful in some circumstances, as might other alternative therapies, but CBT, EMDR and medication are often what is considered best practice. So don't struggle on feeling like crap, do find help, and have the courage to try to switch your treatment if it's not working for you.

I visited a cranial osteopath to realign my spine and soul after I had two miscarriages following my traumatic first birth experience. He said that my uterus seemed to have retained the epidural from my birth two years previously ... I have no idea how on earth he can have discovered this, it's a bit intangible and magic, but he felt he was able to rid my body of the epidural, and seeing him helped me to 'exorcise' any birth demons that my body was insistent on retaining (and preventing any further pregnancy from setting up home there). And it's possibly no coincidence that I became pregnant immediately after and then successfully brought another wonderfully bonkers little boy into the world.

Safe space visualisation exercise

This activity brings you to a safe space so that you can allow yourself some room to just be calm and let go of any anxious thoughts.

Substitute the place for somewhere that resonates with you.

- Imagine you are on the top of a hill at the end of the day.
- You can see the beautiful, red sunset.
- You can see all the houses in the town below.
- You can see small people and cars far below.
- You can smell the fresh air.
- You can feel the cool breeze on your skin.
- It is so peaceful and quiet.
- You feel relaxed.
- Stay as long as you want to, enjoying the peace and quiet.

Five-senses grounding exercise

This exercise can be used to calm yourself in times of stress, or when you find yourself ruminating pointlessly about things that people have said, or are feeling judged or anxious.

It brings you back into the present moment, and is very calming.

1. Sit in a comfortable upright position with your feet planted flat on the ground, or on the floor with your legs crossed. Rest your hands on your thighs.

2. Notice your breath. There's no need to breathe in any particular way; just bring attention to each part of the breath – the inhale, the exhale and the space in between.

3. Bring awareness to each of your five senses, one at a time, for about a minute each. Focus on the *present moment* and how each sense is being activated in that moment.

4. **Hear.** Begin to notice all of the sounds around you. Try not to judge the sounds – just notice them. They are not good or bad, they just are. Sounds might be internal, like your breathing or even your tummy. Sounds could be close by, or more distant like the sound of a plane in the sky. Are you now hearing more than you were before you started? You may begin to notice subtle sounds you didn't hear before. Can you hear them now?

5. **Smell.** Notice the smells of your environment. Maybe it's food? A scented candle? You might become aware of the smell of trees or plants if you are outside. Maybe even books, or paper. Closing your eyes can sharpen your other senses.

6. **See.** Observe your surroundings; notice the colours, shapes and textures.

7. **Taste.** Is there an aftertaste of a drink or meal? Notice your tongue in your mouth, your saliva, your breath. You can run your tongue over your teeth and cheeks.

8. **Touch.** Bring your attention to the sensations of skin contact with your chair, clothing, feet on the floor. Notice the pressure between your feet and the floor, or your body and the chair. Observe temperature, the warmth or coolness of your hands or feet. Take time to feel textures by touching the things within arm's reach.

Postnatal depletion

If you're feeling low in body, this can manifest itself in lowness of spirit as well. In a 2013 article on the website Goop, the supermum's online mecca curated by Gwyneth Paltrow, an Australian GP, Dr Oscar Serrallach, coined the term 'postnatal depletion'. I told a group of five mum friends about it on a (rare) evening drinks night, and everyone around the table said, 'Oh my god, that's totally ME!'

In a nutshell, postnatal depletion affects the postnatal *years*, not just the immediate aftermath of birth. It's a constant sense of fatigue and exhaustion, combined with a feeling of 'baby brain' – or, more accurately, 'child brain' if your baby has long since graduated from that term – as well as poor concentration and 'emotional liability', where your emotions fluctuate like a rollercoaster. A friend of mine calls it her 'leaky egg feeling' – when your runny egg yolk of emotions just keeps spilling everywhere while everyone around you seems hard-boiled and keeping it together.

Other symptoms include:

- feeling tired all the time, falling asleep unintentionally
- hyper vigilance (feeling that your 'radar' is constantly on), anxiety or a sense of unease ('tired and wired')
- guilt and even shame around the role of being a mother ('just' a mum), loss of self-esteem, a sense of isolation and apprehension, fear or anxiety about socialising or leaving the house
- frustration, overwhelm, and a sense of not coping ('There is no time for *me*!')
- no sparkle, or essence ('Who the hell am I?').

Many women from Dr Serrallach's Australian research group said they often 'cried for no reason'. Even a comment like 'crying *for no reason*', which we all say to ourselves, invalidates that we are actually crying for very good reasons, i.e. all of the above! Quite frankly, who wouldn't be crying? And yet we belittle what we are going through, which compounds the feeling of failure.

Combined with this, there is often a feeling of vulnerability, and of not feeling 'good enough'. 'There is plenty of prenatal support,' Oscar Serrallach explains, 'but as soon as a baby is born, the whole focus goes to the baby. There's very little focus on the mother. The mother disappears into the shadows of her role.'

Dr Ellie Cannon, a GP and health columnist, says similarly, 'I think that we are overly prepared for the baby to come. But we are under prepared for the physical and emotional changes that come with a baby. Modern parents think there is an answer to everything on Google. And when the answers don't come neatly packaged they don't know what to do ... Psychologically there is still an expectation that women will take second place to their husband and baby, while their partner's life carries on. Then before women have a chance to fully recover, they are on to baby number two.'

'I felt so overwhelmed by visitors in the first few weeks. They want to see the baby, hold the baby, give advice. Relatives and

close friends seem to view it as their right to get to see the baby as soon as possible. I found this exhausting and it made it more difficult for me to grow into my new role as a mother and bond with my baby. We should have just been allowed to lie in bed together for at least a week, getting to know each other before allowing others in and thinking about entertaining. I also wasn't prepared for all the external pressures and expectations about how you should look after a baby. All the advice and questioning of the way that you choose to parent is exhausting and undermines your confidence.'

Elizabeth, mum of two

'I am an organised person and liked my house in order; having had a c-section I found it difficult not being able to do housework and keep things in order. My husband and family were helpful but I just craved normality. I was so used to having everything in order I did not cope well with the new baby chaos!'

Sadie, midwife and mum of two

Postnatal depression is an accumulation of factors from the pregnancy, delivery and motherhood in general. Many mothers with depletion don't experience depression, but depletion can lend itself to feelings of depression.

Your genuine superpower

Pregnant women are the ultimate supermum alchemists. The internal magic we use to whizz up this amazing new life inside us is the placenta. It also tunes mother to the baby, and baby to the mother – it's like our little walkie-talkie with our little one, a communication line that only we have access to.

During pregnancy, we supply everything that our growing baby needs via the placenta – which is why so many of us become low in iron, zinc, vitamin B12, vitamin B9, iodine and selenium. Our reserves in important omega 3 fats, calcium and iron stores, and specific amino acids from proteins, are also depleted. If we don't focus on ourselves post birth at least sometimes, these reserves are never replenished. Which means our hair, nails, skin, energy levels, ability to absorb nutrients from food, sleep and more are all compromised.

Add to this a sleep-deprived penchant for coffee and biscuits, not drinking enough water, probably not maximising our nutrient intake in our diets ... plus the effects on gut health of the average birth experience – antibiotics and caesareans – all have a negative effect on our gut flora, which may have profound effects on our digestion, absorption of nutrients and, ultimately, our wellbeing. Lingering low-level health issues can have a real effect on your resilience and mental health – probably nothing that would prompt you to go to the doctor, but enough to make you feel a bit crap and very un-supermum.

Many mothers-to-be are already depleted leading up to pregnancy: long working hours, a demanding social life, rush, rush, rush. We're also having babies later in life – mid-30s–40s mums are increasingly common. I had my first at 35 and my second when I was 39 so, with all the anti-ageing will in the world, our 30s bodies are just not as up to the bouncing back from the task as they would've been in our early 20s.

Health after birth

Pregnancy and birth bring physical and psychological changes that partners simply don't have to contend with. But having to, and wanting to, compete on a level playing field with men has made our society squash the effects of childbearing on a woman's constitution, emotions and abilities.

Christina McKenzie, a consultant midwife at Chelsea and Westminster Hospital in London, and a passionate advocate of perinatal mental and physical health, says, 'The modern portrayal of birth is that everyone who goes into pregnancy will come out unscathed. The media and healthcare professionals are a lot to blame. Women expect to come out the same as they went in, and we can't match their expectations.'

This is the key – historically, childbirth has always been an event that has been perceived as high risk. Women used to quite rightly fear giving birth, due to the risk to their or their baby's life. In the early part of the 20th century, it was the second most common cause of death for women of childbearing age, falling only behind TB. Surviving childbirth meant that you just put up with any of the physical issues and problems as a natural side-effect.

Historically in the UK, the medical focus has been slanted towards maternal health over infant health – a sign that in the 19th and 20th centuries, infant mortality rates were much higher. But now that, happily, we are losing fewer babies at birth, and birth has arguably never been 'safer' in the West, it is also sadly true that the health of the mother postnatally has been pushed down the list.

When I worked in central London, I walked past the General Lying-In Hospital every day. I always found the name funny, conjuring up images of ladies lounging around. In fact, a 'lying-in' hospital used to be a maternity hospital, and women were made to 'lie in' in bed for 14 days, without being allowed to leave for fresh air or natural light, so that they would recover fully from the trials of childbirth before being sent back out into society with their newborn.

Now, that recovery time is generally around six hours if you've had a birth without complications. And, let's face it, even if there are no 'complications' with your birth, it has probably been a powerful, painful, immense, formative experience in your life, which you will remember forever. Now that giving birth has become a bit more 'conveyor belt', mothers are really not prepared for the *to-be-expected* physical outcomes that might happen beyond the birth.

Your health is inevitably compromised through pregnancy and childbirth. But our image of Supermum in all her perfection, swanning around with her immaculately blow-dried hair and flat tummy two hours after having her baby, doesn't help us deal with this.

'Closing the bones' ceremony

An ancient Mexican and Ecuadorian tradition, Closing of the Bones is a healing and nourishing ritual for a new mother. It is a ceremony to literally close the body after it has been laid bare and opened, physically and emotionally, by the process of pregnancy and childbirth. The mother is wrapped, massaged with oils, her space blessed. Traditionally, this ceremony is repeated many times in the 40 days after birth: to physically close the hips, pelvis and abdominals, and to nourish the mother's body and spirit, allow her to feel protected and safe at this vulnerable time, encourage circulation to the pelvic organs and stimulate milk production.

This ceremony is being adopted and offered more and more by doulas in the UK to allow mums even years beyond childbirth to enter into a healing journey and release difficult emotions related to the birth.

Chrissie, a mum of two girls who are both school age, experienced the closing the bones ceremony when her youngest was three. She says, 'I do know how ridiculous it sounds but I felt that a great shift had happened inside ... like I released feelings and pent up tensions about my birth and of the last five years of being a mum, and everything felt different, I felt my body had become mine again and I was at peace.'

Other postpartum practices and traditions

Traditionally, women may have had multigenerational support groups for mothers – 'it takes a village'. And these groups have been part of human cultures for millennia, but they're sadly disappearing from our modern culture – particularly in cities, where you could live next door to someone going through exactly what you are but not have any idea.

This is actually a true story for me. When pregnant with my second, I met a lovely mum at pregnancy yoga and we went for a coffee afterwards. We ended up bonding over our shared fear of going through the horrors of the newborn phase again, where we had felt lonely, scared, completely clueless and incompetent. Our firstborns were about the same age. It turns out we lived on the same road. How ridiculous is that? Instead of being able to provide support, tea and friendship for each other, we both went through a horrible experience separately, within shouting distance of each other.

Many mothers suffer in silence like we did, and we're generally not receiving the tapestry of experience, education, guidance and support that tribal mothering culture used to provide. Now, the mother has to be 'everything' from the beginning, to know everything about her child, to be able to do it all.

Postnatal depletion is much more common in modern society these days. Western society has overlooked the fact that mothers need to be fully supported and healthy – physically, emotionally, mentally. All around the world, there have been centuries of practices built around social support networks, to lovingly and collectively restore the normal functioning of the new mother's reproductive organs, promote wound healing, increase wellbeing and energy, and generally look after a new mum's mind, body and spirit. Now, we basically have an isolated practice of a Netflix boxset and a packet of biscuits.

A new mother in Malay villages has 40 days of being looked after by the village women, her abdomen regularly massaged with a paste of ginger, garlic, tamarind and lime, a sash wrapped around her waist to help her to close her abdominals and allow her uterus to shrink. She's given daily hot baths with fragrant leaves, to restore balance and health, and to encourage her milk to flow, before being invited to rejoin the community with her baby.

In traditional Chinese culture, 'doing the month' is observed, whereby the mother doesn't leave the house for 30 days and has no duties apart from breastfeeding the baby. She is fed special 'rebuilding' warm foods such as chicken soup. In Chinese medicine it's believed that pregnancy and birth deplete the body's 'yang' – heat – and everything is done to ensure that balance is restored. The mother is encouraged to stay indoors while her body heals, as to allow cold to enter the body would bring with it long-term health disruption such as rheumatism.

In the 19th century in the UK it was commonplace to have a community midwife taking on a lot of newborn-care duties for a new mother, such as washing nappies, swaddling the baby and soothing it through the night, for the first few weeks. Now, this would be an expensive luxury.

Even our vocabulary reflects our harsh societal standards for the postnatal experience. Beccy Hands, a doula and massage therapist who focuses on postpartum nurturing, trained recently with a group of midwives in Mexico. She was struck by how little nurturing and honouring of the postpartum period we allow in the West compared to what the Mexican midwives were used to. She says, 'the midwives on the course kept referring to "love lines" on our tummy. One of us asked what she meant. Seeing our confused faces she asked what we called them. Her face was full of horror when she realised we called them "stretch marks", "such ugly language!" she cried. Imagine how much better we'd feel about our stripes if we called them "love lines"!'

Create your village

Imagine you are living in your own virtual village.

- What type of residences you would like for your village? Choose structures that suit your personality, e.g. houses, huts, tree dwellings, etc.

- Most importantly, who would you like to have living with you in your village? You might choose some family members, some friends, some work colleagues.

- With your home in the centre, where would your fellow villagers live in relation to you?

- What would everyone's 'village' roles and responsibilities be? You might choose some fellow residents who are good listeners; others might be great entertainers or be able to make you laugh. Perhaps some residents will have skills in helping to organise, clean or cook, while others might make brilliant babysitters.

Just thinking about **being taken care of**, and **delegating roles,** can help clarify exactly how much work daily life involves after having a baby.

In addition, it can help you think about your **networks**. If you notice there are too few other residents or definite skills gaps in your virtual village, this can help clarify what's missing in your real life.

Retrospective guilt

Perhaps you didn't feel a flood of love for your baby initially in that first meeting. Perhaps all you felt was relief, exhaustion, indifference. Sadie, a midwife herself and mum of two, says, 'I had a very difficult labour and birth with my first boy. I was severely anaemic, and very tired and shell-shocked afterwards. I didn't really want to hold him, I just wanted to sleep and recover.'

These emotions are 'normal', so don't allow yourself to feel guilty in retrospect that you weren't the perfect earth mother filled with joyous love for your baby from the moment of birth. The 'perfect mum' with unambiguous emotions simply does not exist in reality.

Amy, a mum of two, had a tricky birth first time round, going into labour at 37 weeks and then struggling so much with feeding that her baby 'failed to thrive' (there's that failure word again, folks) and had to be hospitalised. She says, 'I was a total nutcase. I spent more time looking at my nipple than I did my baby and now feel guilty not that I couldn't exclusively breastfeed, but that I was so obsessed with it, I missed enjoying so many precious moments with my baby.'

The messages we are given about 'best care' (breast is best, etc.) can often get in the way of our being able to trust our gut and get on with what we know is *right for our baby to thrive*, and for us to get on with enjoying motherhood with sanity, and nipples, intact. Amy was intent on her baby thriving – inarguably a sign of a great mother – but felt that she was 'wrong' by not breastfeeding, so allowed this to get in the way of her being able to go with the flow happily.

Ironically she was at her most supermum – caring deeply about how her baby was thriving and doing everything she could do ensure this – when she felt her least. This led to feelings of that annoying mum interloper, guilt – entirely understandable when she thinks she missed out on precious moments.

If this resonates with you, it is worth picking over which events you feel you missed out on that were particularly precious, and what makes/made them so precious to you. A lot of mums have said to me that they have felt they were 'levitating' above their lives in the early baby days, not quite present, not quite absent, just keeping on keeping on, as if watching their lives through mottled glass. It's only in hindsight that they realised how detached they were feeling as they were on survival mode in those exhausted days. And this has led to guilt in retrospect for feeling that they weren't fully there for their baby.

There may be ways to 'make up' for missing out on the baby days with your children now, or you might find that they may not be as important as you first thought, once there has been an opportunity to think them through in a helpful way – which your guilt is currently blocking.

Recapturing blissful moments

ACTIVITY

Use your notebook to help you bring to mind the early bonding experiences you feel are important.

1. Jot down memories of peaceful moments that you can remember from those early days.

2. Write down what you would like to recapture, if you felt you missed anything. It could be that committing to a full 'lovebomb' day with your child now would reclaim some of the tranquillity or connection you felt you missed in those early days.

3. If these missed newborn/baby moments would still have been so important in retrospect, give yourself some time to think about and assemble them now as this can help you to then move on.

Mother's intuition

The modern pressure to be a 'perfect mum', the construct of what makes a 'good mother', has grown in our culture over the past couple of decades. Has this rigid idea of what is 'right' got in the way of 'mother's intuition' or trusting our instincts?

We're told 'how to be a good mother', what we 'should' be doing at each stage. If these guidelines feel at odds with the direction we naturally want to follow, we experience a big dollop of guilt for doing it the 'wrong' way, 'making a rod for your own back', etc.

But the notion of 'right and wrong' is complex. Human relationships are complex and varied, so to expect all babies and children (small humans, remember) to respond evenly to a firm set of guidelines and instructions is leading us to feel like failures. We can separate out the notion of your instinct and frame it as an internal message that allows you to be authentic and true to yourself.

You don't parent the same way your neighbour might, or your sister, even. Even between different children of your own there will be subtle nuances in the ways you respond and shepherd them, because they are different people. So ultimately we need to reject the notion that we are 'getting it wrong' according to arbitrary societal guidelines, and try to get to a point where we can trust that what we are doing is appropriate to *our* child, family and selves.

This is what I mean by 'instincts' when I use this term. Yes, we might need to seek guidance and information and your gut instinct may not always be a strong, sure, glowing beacon – health visitors, websites and books are there to serve a useful purpose, even if it's just to indicate to us what we *don't* agree with. Rather than letting a 'norm', such as 'babies should sleep from 7p.m. to 7a.m. every night', cause us to doubt ourselves, we should use it as a way of noticing the resounding voice inside that tells us that actually we want to go the other way – and not be judged for it.

> *'I compare myself to other mums largely in situations where they have their shit together and I don't! All the mums I met first time round had second babies at the same time as me – and none of them had to move back in with their mum to cope! They are my best support in many ways but a hurtful mirror at times, showing your own inadequacies.'*
> Emma, mum of two

> *'Before you have children you have NO comprehension of the exhaustive nature of being a mother 24/7. But it's not something you can explain to someone before they've had a child – you cannot begin to comprehend how that feels as you've NEVER experienced it before. My baby wouldn't be put down and I felt like I was obviously getting it wrong, as all the books talk about putting your baby down as if it's the easiest thing in the world.'*
> Debbie, mum of two

Maybe we should challenge the dominant accepted narrative of motherhood, challenge our core beliefs in a *productive* way. Instead of thinking, 'I am a failure because I let my baby sleep on my chest for every nap in the first year of her life, when I should have put her down to sleep', we should soften that thought to, 'I followed my instinct that my baby wanted to be close to my heart, decided that her being calm was a good thing, and I soaked up those cuddles without guilt.'

Other models of motherhood

Look further afield and see what motherhood means across the world, across different cultures and countries – in history, even. In this way, recognise how our harsh self-judgements can be turned around positively: 'getting into bad habits' could otherwise be known as 'trusting our instincts'. We might feel like we're a bit rubbish for putting on CBeebies so we can catch up on emails/stare glassily at our phones for a bit, but that's a whole lot better than leaving your crying baby in a pram in the garden for hours, which mums in the 1950s used to be recommended to do so that they could get on with the business of keeping the home.

Esther, a mum of one, works in fashion and had a work trip to Paris. Of course her baby decided to choose that day to wake up feverish and unhappy. The mum-guilt tug of war ensued: work guilt, or baby guilt (more of this meaty subject in Chapter 7). Can't let work down, but, also, my baby is clearly poorly and needs me. So, she followed her gut instinct, scooped her baby up in his pyjamas, put him in a sling, and got on the Eurostar.

She says, 'I pottered around with him all day, he had a lovely time snuggled on my back or sleeping up front, looking at beautiful things and eating croissants. At one point, an African woman came up to me and said "it's so great to see you carrying your baby on your back" ... and it made me think about African traditional cultures, they permanently have their baby on their back as they get on with everyday living, and you rarely see their babies crying. That's because it's normal to carry them around with them everywhere. Their mothers don't rush home for "nap time" because they simply sleep on the go, attached to their mums. Their babies seem so happy and content. This must surely be the most natural thing to do? It made me feel sad that we live in a society where we "need" so much that we have so much work to do and it's distanced ourselves from our instincts.'

Now some of you might read that and not feel an affinity. It's definitely *not* intended as a judgement if you wouldn't ever have dreamt of wearing your baby and preferred to put your baby down for a nap. If I tell you that I still have to lie down with my toddler if I want him to nap during the day, half of you will no doubt be horrified, while others may nod and smile in recognition. The point is that we need to be gentle on ourselves about *what worked for us*, what made the days easier, what allowed us to stay sane – not judge ourselves, or other people, for their choices.

Looking at how some other cultures balance birth and babyhood with 'life rules' shows you that the 'rods for your back' and 'creating a clingy child' mentalities simply don't feature in the cultural dialogue to beat mothers up.

> '*I stopped giving my daughter a bottle at a year, just refused to give it to her any more as I read that she should be having only a sippy cup from then on. She was so distraught and it was really horrible for ages. Looking back, I wonder why I didn't just carry on giving her a bottle, because it made her happy, and we used to have a lovely time cuddling while she had her milk, which then stopped as she hated the sippy cup. But I felt I had to do the "right thing", and I had read that that was the right thing.'*
>
> Jo, mum of one

Were there times when you felt you'd got it so 'wrong' because your baby didn't sleep through the night in a Moses basket but instead wanted constant kangaroo care next to your chest? Something that is labelled 'bad practice' in one culture is embraced as entirely normal in another.

Your 'ideal mum' belief system can be questioned by looking at motherhood around the world. This might actually help you to reconcile yourself to your own practices, even if they are not 'cultural norms' for your immediate society – co-sleeping, prolonged breastfeeding, etc. You're going with your instinct.

Similarly, did you want to follow an attachment-parenting vibe but felt like you failed to do it 'properly' because at times you craved space and distance from your boob-hungry toddler? If you desperately needed a full night's sleep to prevent yourself from becoming a devil woman and so had to sleep train, cut yourself some slack. Coping with broken sleep when you work full time, and breastfeeding your baby until age five, in our modern society just *isn't that easy*. You're doing the best you can. You have to be realistic about what you can achieve while also maintaining a balance for yourself.

There is a deep tradition in other cultures of nurturing mums and honouring the enormous physical and emotional feat that we have performed by carrying a person in our womb and giving birth – whereas in our culture we are all about getting back to HIIT classes or fitting into skinny jeans as soon as possible, without admitting that you actually feel a bit pummelled. You've experienced something that has changed you intrinsically, seismically, forever. It's OK to admit that maybe it would've been nice to have someone hold you gently for a fourth trimester, as if in a cocoon, while you transition into your new form as a mother butterfly.

> 'It is a time of amazing intensity and massive adjustment. Your body transforms – again – and your heart throbs with more feelings than you ever knew possible … days and nights merge. Your stamina and serenity get tested like never before. Your connections to the world you knew before loosen, or even come undone, and your sense of who you are begins to change and morph.'
>
> Heng Ou, The First Forty Days

4

Finding your mojo: 'Where's my brain? I'm so fricking tired. Who am I?'

This chapter walks us through how we need to crystallise our identities as mums. It offers strategies for celebrating the mum person that we have turned into while simultaneously embracing parts of our former selves – and perhaps waving a fond goodbye to others.

Do you have days when you wake up, look in the mirror, and wonder where you've gone? Where did she go, that funny, vivacious, confident woman? The one who used to wear sequins, not just to the school disco. I miss her – she was great fun. Supermum never has a crisis of confidence or identity. She manages to strike the right balance between mum time and me time without ever feeling guilty. Supermum's relationship is effervescent with chemistry, never affected by the 'oh gaaad, please let me sleep and have no one touch me for a moment!' effects of small children on a relationship. Supermum never questions her essence or thinks, 'hang on, where the HELL has my mojo gone?'

Supermum is a figment of our imaginations, a she's-doing-it-much-better-than-me stick to beat ourselves with. This chapter will take you through how there is a monumental sea change that takes over us when we become mothers, which causes us to lose sight of who we were before and start drifting along without being anchored to any sense of self or purpose. We'll look at how and why this happens, and see how *normal and common* it is – if you were to fight your shyness and strike up a conversation with another mum at the playground about it, I'm pretty sure you would be united in your common mourning of your ability to remember what your middle name is sometimes.

This chapter explores ways of igniting and reconnecting to your mojo, working through some therapies to uncover what's blocking it, and offers you some self-care strategies that will help to put *you* back on your to-do list.

Mothermorphosis

The transition to motherhood is like going through a one-way turnstile: you can look back at where you came from, but you can't ever pass back to that place.

Kate Figes, in *Life After Birth*, says, 'Every woman who gives birth needs an extensive period to come to terms with the irrevocable changes to her body so that she can more easily accept her new role as a mother. There are billions of tiny lights glowing inside each one of us, and it can feel as if the effort it takes to produce each child is so great that it extinguishes a few of those lights forever. We can live perfectly well without them, but that does not mean that we do not need time to mourn their loss.'

It's the mourning of their loss that we don't do brilliantly. We don't treat this time as the real metamorphosis we should – leaving part of ourselves behind and transitioning to a new way of living life: becoming a mother, therefore a *completely new person*. We can end up in a bit of a cul-de-sac of latent malaise that we're not sure what to do with but it sure steals our sparkle. There are mixed feelings involved with leaving parts of your old self behind, but it's not something we're really encouraged to dwell on – having a baby is happy and joyous, full stop.

Nowadays we have a culture of carrying on as normal after birth, arguably dismissing the hugeness of creating a new life: expecting to be exactly the same, physically and mentally, coming out the other end of it. Surely this expectation that we'll emerge unchanged from the experience is just setting us all up for feeling silently like we're not coping, that we're failing because we haven't managed it and (we assume) everyone else is fine?

> 'A friend had told me that being in labour felt like being murdered, and I loved that honesty – she was right ... and I was actually pleased to be prepared for how awful it'd feel.'
>
> Natalie, mum of two

> 'Nobody tells you. And then you, in turn, don't tell anyone. You can't describe it. Motherhood is weird, strange, horrible, magic, wonderful. How can you actually tell anyone what it's like?'
>
> Hollie, mum of one

I assumed that after birth I would simply have to lose a bit of podge. I didn't have any real understanding that I would have undergone such a seismic alteration that it was almost as if I had stepped into an entirely new body suit, one that didn't really fit yet and might not for a few years.

The return of your mojo is the magical period when the 'old childless you' and the 'mummy you' finally harmonise, like yin and yang; instead of a push-me-pull-you of not knowing exactly who you are any more, you soften into your new identity and fully embrace it, no longer notice it not 'fitting'.

Your physiology, metabolism, hormone levels, respiratory and digestive systems – every system of the body – are challenged *and altered* by pregnancy and childbirth, not to mention the continued hormonal surges thereafter that resonate like aftershocks of an earthquake. And yet we're still expected to be back in our skinny jeans and jumping on trampolines merrily as soon as we can.

What is normal, anyway?

I saw a good friend when her first baby was six weeks old. Wide-eyed with sleep deprivation in those visceral early days, she said, 'I just really need things to get back to normal a bit. When does it start getting back to *normal?*' Erm ... never? This can be a common desire in new motherhood, and a constant quest thereafter.

Motherhood contains so many passing phases, so much change and development, transition, that we keep having to create a new normal. Each phase by turns is easier, harder, more challenging, allows more sleep, less sleep. It requires you to recalibrate and redefine yourself at each turn, find a new rhythm.

The transience of each new 'normal' means that we're constantly responding to external factors – fighting fires, rather than having a semblance of autonomy over the direction our life is steered in as we may have done before our hearts were beating outside our bodies. If we hold on to a supermum vision of perfection, we might feel like we're falling short of attaining that equilibrium; as if we're constantly trying to chase a butterfly and catch it rather than being able to sit comfortably still and allow it to settle on us.

> 'When my baby was around ten months old I finally felt like I had got to a feeling of normality ... up until then I was always feeling chaotic, trying to remember everything before I left the house and always forgetting at least one thing: wipes, bottle, nappies, baby ...?! And then one day I realised I had gone out to the park with him and it didn't feel like a struggle, and that's when I thought, actually maybe I'm getting the hang of this.'
>
> Ayo, mum of one

> 'Discovering who I really am has been the biggest lesson of having my children – motherhood is the biggest self-reveal there is.'
>
> Hannah, mum of two

Just keep swimming

Mums often talk about being in 'survival mode' in the first years of motherhood. Of just battening down the hatches to get through the days and weeks with the constant onslaught of children's lurgies, A&E trips, sleepless nights, moodiness and uncertainty about any given phase lasting very long.

Missing your old life with a kind of nostalgia that at times feels like a physical ache, missing *who you were*, and the ability to just nip out to the shops/to the pub with your partner without military planning and dogged determination, can feel like even more of a shock because as a society we perpetuate the myth of the perfect supermum happily breezing through all of this.

> *'I wish I had understood that motherhood was not going to be this breeze, that although it's not a difficult thing to love this other little person, it's difficult to find the energy and time to love yourself when you're giving so much of yourself to that other person.'*
>
> Becky, mum of one

Motherhood is immensely draining on your physical and mental wellbeing, and you need to take steps to protect yourself – you can't pour from an empty cup, the saying goes. But how many of us prioritise self-care? Instead of feeling like everyone else is coping fine, we need to be more honest, strip off the supermum suit and realise that *we are all feeling the same way.* Motherhood is fantastically levelling in this respect.

Even Victoria Beckham must have had moments when her baby vommed in her hair and her toddler called her a smelly poo poo head; when she cried on her chaise longue in her Louboutins and felt like giving up. But, viewed from our little bubble, instead we think that everyone else is coping and we aren't.

When my second was about six weeks old I started going to mum and baby yoga, which I hadn't done with my first as he spent too much time screaming like a banshee and I figured that might wreck the zen in the room (I know now that I should have just taken him along anyway and I would have seen that every baby wrecks the zen in the room at some point: this is a baby's prerogative). But my second was a bit more chilled out (due entirely to my supreme mothering skills, of course).

One week I went with a new mum friend, and she brought along her neighbour. As far as I was concerned, I spent the time juggling attempts to feed my baby in between Warrior poses, feeling flustered, then elated when he fell asleep for five minutes and allowed me to breathe and do a tiny bit of vinyasa flow for myself before he started crying again. I would have described myself as a bit of a shambles that day.

A few days later, my friend told me that her mum pal had been 'in awe of' me because of my 'neat toenail polish'. It just goes to show that others pick out shining lights about you in the face of motherhood craziness that you wouldn't in a million years think of as being worthy of note or celebration because you scrutinise yourself much too closely with your negative glasses on.

Natural 'maternal instinct'

Hannah, a mum of two, told me of her panic in the early days: 'because the research I'd done was all about pregnancy and labour, I hadn't actually learnt anything about having a newborn. Even at the NCT groups, the tutor assumed that it was the men who hadn't changed a nappy so they got to practise, whereas actually I hadn't either! I cried the whole way home in the car, because I was so terrified we would f*ck up and this tiny precious thing would die in our care.'

We touched on instinct and intuition in Chapter 3. As mums, we're supposed to know *instinctively* what to do, and only the man has the right to be clueless (according to stereotypical assumptions). But in modern life we're increasingly distanced from our instincts, and not offered the community and familial support networks that have historically passed down that 'innate' knowledge. Instead, we have a surfeit of parenting books/websites/forums, which offer disparate and contradictory guidelines ... and make us want to tear our hair out. When our babies settle for Dad/Gran/any random stranger and not us, it can feel like the worst form of incompetence on our part.

> *'I was totally prepared for new motherhood in the sense that I'd been a midwife for seven years prior to having my own baby. I knew about the sleepless nights and I had endlessly settled babies for mums. I had held mums' hands through labour and birth and the early emotional days, I had supported mums with anxiety and depression, I had seen it all. I knew it all. But living it and feeling it was a totally different thing! Knowing everything I was going through was normal and that I wasn't alone made it*

easier to cope with in a way, but it was still relentlessly tiring and chaotic and messy, which doesn't suit my personality!'

Sadie, mum of two and midwife

'When I was pregnant for the first time, I assumed there would be a little voice in my head – a maternal "instinct" – that would explain how best to bathe, feed, care for my newborn, how to get her to sleep. I would just "know". Throughout my pregnancy, worryingly that voice remained silent. I didn't know what was or wasn't "normal". And, of course, I expected that my body would know how give birth ("You're designed for it!"). It absolutely did not.'

Melissa, mum of two

We can feel like a failure if this magic Mary Poppins voice of instinct doesn't sail down immediately and provide us with all the answers. But we need to look at our mum selves as the tortoise, not the hare: slowly and steadily figuring things out as we meander along the mothering road. When our gut feeling does point us in the right direction and we solve a problem – be it an inexplicable toddler meltdown or an approach to getting our child to engage with home learning – we feel so powerful, so wise, so knowing, so smug. But it might not work every time, and this is life. The idea of a foolproof mothering instinct may be as mythical as Supermum herself.

Some of us have to learn everything slowly and painfully, through trial and error, through extensive research. 'You are the expert on your child' – yes, there are absolutely things only you know about your children: their particular likes and dislikes, how long it takes them to get used to new environments, what food they will always reject. But to soften your expectation of your supermum instinct you need to realise that it may not sing out loud all the time, and it's OK to feel a bit lost sometimes.

When you do feel lost, consider all the possibilities, write things down, weigh the pros against the cons, and find a solution that truly feels right and *works in your circumstances* – knowing that you can adapt or discard it if it turns out not to be the right thing further down the line. Maybe we do need to consult various voices sometimes: ask family, friends and (heaven forbid) online forums. It might be that the more information you have, the more you can understand what you actually feel about it and find a fitting solution for you.

We need some external input to help us to learn or develop. This is similar to proximal development, or 'scaffolding learning', used in education. Scaffolding refers to a variety of teaching techniques that offer temporary support and assistance to move students progressively toward stronger understanding and, ultimately, greater independence in the learning process.

Like physical scaffolding, the supportive strategies are incrementally removed when they're no longer needed, and the teacher gradually shifts more responsibility for the learning process over to the student.

So, often, it is valuable to seek external guidance and support. But too much information, especially if it is not being scaffolded well enough for us to take on board, and is too far out of our reach, will make us feel overwhelmed and despondent.

Your mum brain

It's official, folks: having children really does alter your brain cells. Research published in 2016 in the *New Scientist* revealed that the brain is 'pruned' to reinforce the mother's attunement to her newborn. 'I think any mother would intuitively know that they "feel different" after birth', says Liisa Galea at the University of British Columbia in Canada. 'There's an old adage: "once a mother, always a mother", and this research bears this out by showing that a maternal brain is different for at least two years post-pregnancy.'

Dr Oscar Serrallach, inventor of the term 'postnatal depletion', says: 'Part of the job of the placenta is to reprogram the mother. It's as though she gets a "software upgrade", with some parts of the brain being reinforced and other parts of the brain being lessened. The average brain shrinkage during pregnancy is about 5%, but it is not so much the brain getting smaller, but rather being modified to acquire the skills to become a mother. This is not discussed or respected enough in our society: mothers need much support and acknowledgement for this new phase of life.'

Along with our baby in our womb, we develop a 'baby radar', which enables us to become intuitively aware of our child's needs – that state of immediately jumping awake at any flicker of a sound, and constantly hearing your baby crying when you're in the shower, even if baby is out with Dad. This hyper vigilance is obviously vital for our babies in those early days, but without being able to switch it off, and without the right support around us, it can lead to longer-term self-doubt, insecurity and feelings of unworthiness. Modern society has basically created lonely, overwhelmed mothers.

ACTIVITY

Body scan

Sometimes we need to connect back to our body.

This exercise should take about 15–20 minutes. Read through the steps before you start, and try to memorise most of them. It may take a few attempts to able to do the whole exercise with your eyes closed, without referring to the instructions.

Lie on the floor on a mat, making sure you are warm and comfortable. Cover yourself with a blanket and rest your head on a cushion or pillow. You can also do this sitting upright, propped up with cushions if necessary.

Slowly, mentally scan your body for any areas of stress, tension or discomfort. Breathe softly throughout, inhaling for a count of five, exhaling for a count of six. If your mind wanders into thinking, planning, worrying or daydreaming, then just gently guide it back to settle on your body.

1. Check in with your body. Notice any sensations that are present, feeling the contact you're making with the floor. Grow heavy.

2. Shift your awareness through different parts of the body, bringing attention to each part, moment to moment.

3. Start with the crown of the head, noticing any sensations here: tingling, tightness? Then bring your awareness to the head, allowing it to feel heavy as it rests on the cushion. Then the forehead, noticing whether or not you can feel your pulse, whether there is tightness. Soften your forehead to free it from tension. Soften the eyes in their sockets, your nose, cheeks, mouth and jaw. Release the tongue from the roof of your mouth. Relax your

ears, noticing any sounds that come into your consciousness. Be aware of any sensations, softness, tension. Notice if your mind is wandering. Be aware of wandering, and gently guide your mind back to the part of the body you are focusing on.

4. Move your awareness into the neck and shoulders, releasing any tension there. As you breathe, feel the air moving into the back of the throat; notice if it's cool or warm.

5. Become aware of your shoulders. Feel the connection between the shoulders and the floor. Allow your shoulder blades to spread open like wings, softening your heart centre. Slowly move your awareness into your arms, elbows, wrists, hands and fingertips.

6. As you continue to breathe, notice the gentle rise and fall of the chest with the in and out breath, turning your awareness to the ribcage, front and back of the ribs, sides of the ribs, the upper back resting on the floor. Notice any aches and pains, any tension or tightness. Breathe a sense of gentleness to these areas.

7. Breathe into your abdomen, and allow it to open and soften. This is where we experience our 'gut feeling'. Notice your attitude to your belly, where you grew your baby, seeing if you can allow it to *be* as it is. Be relaxed, loving and accepting. Then, bring your awareness to the lower back, the lumbar spine, feeling the gentle pressure as the back meets the floor, before moving your awareness to the pelvis, the hip bones and sit bones. Notice any sensations here; send your breath to this area. Try to soften and release any tension.

8. Move your attention into the thighs, feeling the weight of the legs, gently noticing what other sensations there are here. Feel the thigh bones heavy in their sockets.

9. Turn your attention gently towards your knees, your calves: notice how your muscles feel. Now your feet: the heels, the ball of your foot, the tops of the feet, skin and bone. Connect individually to all ten toes. Allow any tension to soften and release.

10. Take one or two slow, deeper breaths, fill your whole body with awareness, noticing any sensations present. Sweep the body with your awareness from top to bottom. Notice whether there is any feeling of non-acceptance towards any parts of the body. Try to fill your body with a gentle awareness; see if you can have gratitude

and compassion rather than negative judgements. Feel the energy of your breath and life flowing through you. Rest in your awareness of this amazing body that you have, compassion for its experiences, its achievements, and appreciation for its capabilities and the wonder of having created a human.

Let's talk about sex, baby

Let's face it, children sap the va-va-voom right out of you. I know one mum who hasn't done the business since her second child was born, two years ago. The sheer physicality of motherhood can make you feel like you're constantly being pulled at or climbed on, pushing something, wrestling someone, lifting something. Not to mention, with small children particularly, the abundance of kisses and cuddles that you get, and give – filling your love cup to the brim. So to have someone else demand more physicality from you at the end of a day can sometimes be dismissed with a frosty resistance.

In my Pilates studio I run monthly Mothers' Wellness Evenings with a hypnobirthing practitioner, where we get a group of local mums together for some Pilates, breathing, a general chat and activities based around life coaching and NLP (neuro-linguistic programming). One topic that always comes up is the lack of mojo being more apparent in the bedroom than anywhere else.

Kirsty, a mum of two school-age children, said, 'I almost avoid any physical contact because I'm a bit worried it's going to give my husband ideas, so I shy away from hugs or any kind of contact in case he gets the wrong idea.' Sophie agreed, 'because I don't want to "encourage" anything I seem to completely withdraw from any kind of physical tenderness. I know it's made my partner sad, and it makes me really sad too.' Alison simply said, 'I used to love kissing. Now I never ever do it as the idea of what it leads to is simply not worth the energy I have available.'

Ayelet Waldman, in *Bad Mother*, puts it brilliantly: 'I would sooner have leaped into a tank full of starving great whites, while having my period, than have sex. Whatever sensual satisfaction I needed was amply provided by my sweet-smelling, plump, and delicious baby ... Even after the hormone flood had ebbed, breastfeeding was enough to keep me from wanting any other physical contact. I spent my days and nights at the baby's beck and call, my body and breasts available whenever the baby wanted them. The last thing I could tolerate in the few hours I had my body to myself was to give it to someone else.'

There is not enough recognition that, although clearly both parents go through a huge shift in lifestyle priorities and learn to survive on much less sleep, the birth mother has to contend with a whole load of physical changes that place on the body the equivalent stress of trekking to reach a mountain summit, or completing a triathlon, without the chance to sleep and recuperate afterwards.

Men (or a female partner who hasn't been through pregnancy) are affected differently by having babies: their brains and bodies are simply not altered like ours are. On some level, in order to preserve your relationship, we need to start to see their point of view and try to move towards a middle ground.

So, get support. Create a babysitting circle of friends who reciprocate sitting offers. Commit to having time at least once a month when you and your partner just hang out, make eye contact, touch, flirt, hug, have a glass of wine or a coffee together, and communicate.

The importance of sleep

We might not be getting frisky at night, but we're definitely not sleeping much. We talked about postnatal depletion in the previous chapter. Fatigue is the most common symptom in postnatal depletion, and it's definitely something that becomes worse as a result of accumulated mum-stress/lack of sleep. Research published in 2016 by the Children's Sleep Charity and Netmums revealed that a quarter of parents reported that lack of sleep affected their wellbeing, mental health and relationship. More than half admitted that they're *only pretending to cope* with the long-term sleep deprivation. Hello, Supermums! The study revealed that:

- 56% of parents said that their child/children wake up once, twice, three times or more during any one night
- 35% said they are regularly sleep deprived and exhausted

- 22% said that a lack of sleep had an effect on their relationship with their partner
- 17% said their partner is regularly sleep deprived and exhausted.

The quest for vitality and boundless energy requires a magical mix of the right amounts of sleep, exercise, fun, and a diet packed full of nutrients: iron, vitamin B12, zinc, vitamin C, vitamin D ... but it also just requires your little buggers to go to bed and sleep all night. And sometimes they don't and it's out of your control. But, you've got to start somewhere – so even if your children are the main spanner in your sleeping works, try the following tips for enhancing your chances of a good night's kip.

- Create a night-time ritual: what you do in the hour before sleep can make a huge difference to the quality of your rest. Expose yourself only to soft yellow/orange lighting (i.e. no computer, smartphone or TV screens) and a soothing environment (as much as your children allow ...)
- Don't drink any caffeine in the afternoon, and avoid too much alcohol, as this disrupts your sleep. Sorry, wine-o-clock ritual ...
- Have magnesium salt baths before bed – mineral deficiency can have a huge impact on our health, and absorbing magnesium through the skin is the most effective way of doing it. A hot bath is a wonderful way of relaxing. Win–win.
- Treat your bedroom as an oasis of calm. If there is one room that you need to keep tidy and clutter-free in your house, it should be the bedroom (author looks at 'chair of shame' and hangs head meekly).
- Keep your bedroom as cool, quiet and dark as possible. Limit the amount of electronic gadgets you have plugged in there.

'Exhaustion is the worst thing about motherhood for sure. That mean bugger can make even the strongest of souls question their abilities.'

Alex, single mum of one

'I used to get very stressed about their sleep. Neither of them sleep through the night yet, which is unusual compared with

other children it seems. I would feel embarrassed to admit this to other mothers who might complain that their six-month-old doesn't sleep through, when my toddlers still don't.'

Elizabeth, mum of two

'I think the tiredness is the biggest thing for me – if someone could take that away and if I could have a good night's sleep every night I think I could cope with everything else. The tiredness makes me into a pretty horrible person. I cry, I am ratty, negative, paranoid, angry. I swear a lot when I am tired. I have such a short fuse sometimes. It's like you know you have this precious experience every day to enjoy and you are just too damned tired to enjoy it. It feels such a waste. So when people tell you their baby sleeps well and they're not tired, it is a really big deal to me. It is like they are telling me that they enjoy being a mother and they enjoy their children much more than I do. For me, not enjoying things enough is the stick I beat myself with.

I really don't beat myself up much about whether my house is tidy enough, whether I dress nicely enough, do I look OK, are my children dressed in perfectly coordinated Boden outfits, are they eating perfectly designed and made with love Annabel Karmel meals, is their bedroom Pinterest worthy (although I would be lying if every one of these anxieties hasn't made its way into my worry list at some point), but these things have never been a problem big enough to turn on the waterworks. What I really struggle with is whether I am enjoying it all enough because I'm so bloody exhausted.'

Kelly, mum of two.

Research shows that sleep deprivation can cause:

- memory problems
- low mood
- increased anxiety
- weight gain and digestive issues
- weakened immune system.

'Sleep is the big thing. All the sleep training books just make you feel like a failure when your baby only naps for ten minutes and wakes 236 times in the night.'

Natalie, mum of two

'Tiredness before kids was only ever short lived as you could catch up on sleep. You had personal time (or, just "time", then) to wash, go to the toilet – all the things you did not even consider a luxury before that baby arrived.'

Debbie, mum of two

So, what can you do to set your inner supermum free when she's trapped in your lethargic sleepy body? Here are some self-care tips for creating energy on those days when the life has been sapped out of you.

Dry body brushing

You may be thinking, why are you telling me to add something else to my already crazy morning routine? Well, the extra three minutes this takes is well worth the investment. I do it before I jump in the shower. Start at your feet and brush upwards, towards the heart. It's said to boost circulation, sweep away dead skin cells, stimulate the lymph nodes, help digestion and improve the appearance of cellulite. But, more importantly, it *wakes you up* and makes you feel more positive.

Pranayama breathing technique

This yoga breathing technique is called *Nadi Shodhana*, or alternate nostril breath. It helps clear out blocked energy channels in the body, which in turn calms the mind. To be honest, simply focusing on any type of deep, regular breathing such as the calming breath on pages 37 and 108 will help. But this yoga breathing technique will particularly energise and revitalise you, and help keep your mind calm, happy and peaceful. A few minutes of Nadi Shodhana pranayama in a day de-stresses the mind and releases fatigue. Tick.

- Sit comfortably with your spine tall and shoulders relaxed.
- Place your left hand on the left knee.
- Place the tips of the index finger and middle finger of the right hand in between the eyebrows, the ring finger and little finger on the left

nostril, and the thumb on the right nostril. We'll use the ring finger and little finger to open or close the left nostril, and thumb for the right nostril.

- Press your thumb down on the right nostril and breathe out gently through the left nostril.
- Now breathe in from the left nostril, and then press the left nostril gently with the ring finger and little finger. Removing the right thumb from the right nostril, breathe out from the right.
- Breathe in from the right nostril and exhale from the left. This is one round. Continue inhaling and exhaling from alternate nostrils.
- Complete nine more rounds, alternately breathing through both the nostrils. After every exhalation, remember to breathe in through the same nostril from which you exhaled. Keep your eyes closed throughout and continue taking long, deep, smooth breaths without any force or effort.

Facial massage: tapping; massaging ears

This may look totally bonkers, but believe me it works. Tap the crown of your head with your fingers, drum them like galloping hooves, quite strongly. Then, massage all around your earlobes and tips of your ears. If you have more time (and are not at work ...), give yourself a bit of a facial massage with a lovely facial oil, which will boost your circulation and give you a rosy glow, plus make you feel awake.

Your posture

Feeling sluggish and crappy simply isn't helped by sitting a lot and not moving enough. I'm a Pilates teacher and so posture is my business – as mums, our posture is affected by forward-hunching activities: pushing buggies, carrying or permanently leaning down to talk to your children, picking up endless debris from the floor, changing nappies – not to mention, added to that, possibly being hunched over a computer at a desk all day. Your state of mind is often reflected in your posture: when your shoulders are slumped, you are squashing your heart and spirit. If you're feeling low, your appearance will be droopy.

Imagine Supermum in an actual superhero costume – she's standing very tall and confident, powerful, right? Picture a Wonder Woman stance. Now try it. Stand up tall, relax your shoulder blades into your back, imagine a bunch of balloons drawing the crown of your head up to the sky, and imagine your heart shining out through your chest. Place your hands on your hips to feel strong and empowered. Then stretch, reach up and lengthen your spine. This really will make you feel more alert, alive and energised.

Commit to a regular yoga or Pilates class and you will also get to feel a glowing sense of achievement – congratulate yourself for doing something to improve your own wellbeing, which will benefit everyone around you as well. There are more examples of this, in 'Finding flow' on page 114.

Getting outside in green space

Natural light and green space have a positive effect on your mental energy. So if you're feeling lacklustre and exhausted, take a short walk in a park, or anywhere that you can see greenery/trees, etc. Breathe in fresh air. Research conducted by the charity Mind said that 'green exercise' improved mental health and encouraged a sense of wellbeing. Being outside – with green space, fresh air, nature, unfamiliar sights and sounds – stimulates your body and mind.

Also be mindful that seasons take their toll – if you're feeling low and it's winter, chances are you haven't had much natural light. Referrals for mental health conditions increase over the winter months. Try to get outside under the gaze of the sun as much as you can, all year round.

ACTIVITY

Diaphragmatic breathing – calming breath

Tapping into your calming breath is a technique that helps you slow down your breathing when you are feeling stressed or anxious.

Newborn babies naturally breathe this way, and so do yogis. So join this chilled-out tribe and learn how to do it for yourself. It's a great tool for those moments when things are getting on top of you. (You can even do it when children are climbing on you and all is chaos around – I've tried.)

When we're feeling anxious or overwhelmed, we tend to take short, quick, shallow breaths. Calming your breath involves taking smooth, slow, regular breaths, which in turn calms your mind and helps you feel more peaceful. Sitting upright with a lengthened torso is a good way of finding your calming breath, as you can increase the capacity of your lungs to fill with air.

1. Take a slow breath in through the nose, breathing into your lower belly, for a count of five.

2. Hold your breath for one or two seconds. Pause and notice that space between the in breath and the out breath. Don't question it or judge it, just notice and observe that stasis.

3. Exhale slowly through the mouth, as if you're sighing or trying to fog a window in front of you, for a count of six.

4. Pause and observe the space between the exhale and the next inhale.

Follow the above steps for at least five breaths. Then:

1. Soften your jaw, your cheeks, your forehead. Then imagine a softness travelling down the base of the neck, into the shoulders, down the spine and into the pelvis, taking any fear or tension away with it. Allow your body to feel peaceful and light.

2. Try to breathe into your diaphragm or belly. Your shoulders and chest should be serene and still. If this is really tricky sitting up, try first lying down on the floor with one hand on your heart, the other on your abdomen. Feel the hand on your tummy rise as you fill your lungs with air. The hand over your heart should barely move, if at all.

Learn to love your body

Let's face it: the way we feel about our bodies can seriously affect our self-esteem and sense of identity, even without having children. After giving birth, we may not recognise our bodies any more. There is immense pressure to 'bounce back' and be back in your pre-pregnancy clothes within hours of having your baby, so if it takes you years it can really start to get you down. Here, we need a reality check. What does it take to get that celebrity body post-baby in real life?

Post-children, your body might feel like you're living in the same house but with all the rooms in the wrong place. Ultimately there has to be an acceptance that some of the changes caused by giving birth are permanent. I have a lovely c-section overhang, a result of the way my surgery was pinned, which will never go away, no matter how much Pilates I do. I sometimes touch it and feel a huge sense of sadness and loss. But you need to flip this feeling around. It's not going anywhere, so you must accept it. In our society we're conditioned to be dissatisfied with the way we look. But stop and remember that *it's OK to love your body*. You're allowed.

Be open and honest if you are feeling physically under par. I've spoken to women who feel, *years* after they've had their children, that things still aren't right 'down there'. You might be avoiding sex as it's uncomfortable, you might feel like it doesn't feel 'normal' but you're just putting up with it. Understand that your feelings are important and legitimate, and have the confidence to press your GP.

You could be referred to a women's health physiotherapist to help address issues that your birth might have created. Talk more about this openly with other mums, in a way that feels comfortable for you, and you may start to discover a) that others have similar things going on, and b) when something is definitely *not* worth putting up with.

ACTIVITY

Progressive muscle-relaxation exercise

We mums are often so tense throughout the day that we don't even recognise what being relaxed feels like. Learn to detect how your body is really feeling, and to be able to release tension.

Progressive muscle relaxation teaches you how to relax your muscles in two steps. First, you tense particular muscle groups in your body, such as your neck and shoulders. Then, you release the tension and notice how your muscles feel when you relax them. This exercise will help you to lower your overall tension and stress levels, and help you relax when you are feeling anxious. It can also help reduce physical problems such as headaches, as well as improve your sleep.

Through practice, you can learn to distinguish between a tense muscle and a completely relaxed muscle. You can imprint how this feels in your mind. Then, you can begin to 'cue' this relaxed state at the first sign of muscle tension, which might accompany feelings such as anxiety. By tensing and releasing, you learn not only what relaxation feels like, but also to recognise when you are starting to get tense during the day.

Set aside at least 15 minutes, and find a place where you can complete this exercise without being disturbed.

Tense your muscles

- Focus on a muscle group, e.g. your left hand.
- Take a slow, deep breath and squeeze the muscles as hard as you can for about five seconds. (In this example, you're making a tight fist with your left hand.)
- Really feel the tension, which may cause discomfort or even shaking.
- It is easy to accidentally tense other surrounding muscles (e.g. the shoulder or arm, or your face), so try to isolate the muscles you are targeting. This gets easier with practice.

Relax your muscles

- After about five seconds of tensing, let all the tightness flow out. Breathe out as you do this.
- You should feel the muscles become loose and soft, as the tension releases. Focus on and *notice the difference* between the tension and relaxation.
- Remain in a relaxed state for about 15 seconds.

Repeat

- Move on to the next muscle group and repeat the tension–relaxation steps.
- Start with your feet and move up through the body. Remember to repeat on each side of your body.
- At the end of the activity, take a deep breath in through your nose. Hold your breath for a few seconds, then breathe out through your mouth. Breathe deeply at least ten times.

Tummy troubles

As well as issues 'down below', one of the main problems that I encounter with my postnatal Pilates clients is diastasis recti: abdominal separation. Your tummy muscles 'split' to accommodate your growing bump – it also happens to men with big beer bellies. But the muscles don't necessarily zip themselves up again without help, and too many women have no idea that they have a separation – it's still not often something that midwives and GPs give us any information about during pregnancy – and so, in this ignorance, we end up making it worse by trying to do loads of bootcamp sit-ups for that elusive flat tummy.

If you feel, even years after being pregnant, that you still have a jelly belly and look about four months pregnant, get yourself checked by a physio or Pilates teacher. It's never too late to get help to sort it out.

Case study: Abdominal separation

Abdominal separation can wreak havoc on your self-esteem, your posture, your wellbeing. It's a completely normal and natural result of pregnancy but as yet still something we generally don't hear enough about, and therefore we aren't equipped for dealing with it effectively. Mum-of-two Hannah's experience shows us that you need to take action if you feel that your 'mum tum' isn't normal for you, and listen to your body: if you know that something is not right, explore what you can do to rectify it in order to move forward with your life.

'Nearly three months after I'd had my first baby, I'd lost all my self-confidence and wore dark, dreary long-sleeved T-shirts and my maternity jeans because my belly was still so huge. I felt my body was a lost cause, and I gave up on it. My husband was so supportive throughout the whole process, except it took him ages to appreciate the change having a baby had had on my life – we were a sociable couple and he carried on being the sociable one, which meant that we'd be out on a Saturday afternoon and more often than not I ended up taking the baby home to put him to bed while he carried on partying. That caused friction and it took ages for us to reach an equilibrium about it.

'Six months later and my bump still hadn't improved, making me look like I was four to five months pregnant. I found this really distressing, not helped by a friend asking what was going to come out of there next (she was drunk and deeply unhappy in her relationship and so I don't hold it against her, but to this day she has no idea of the impact of her words). I went to a doctor and showed her my belly, asking if it was going to get better. She asked if I'd done any exercise. I started running. I found this to be such a great reliever of stress but more than anything, it was time on my own, moving at my own pace, going where I wanted to go.

'I went back to work after a year, still deeply conscious of my very changed body, and battled with a long commute and a daily punishment from my child when I got home.

'I had two miscarriages and eventually got pregnant again early 2011. My pregnancy second time round was of course different, I was thankful for every day that I held on to the baby, feeling like my body had already failed me twice (or had I failed it?) and eventually was induced at 41 weeks, having a relatively quick and very positive birth experience.

'My belly was by now totally f*cked. Not only did I still look four months pregnant, I had lots of spare skin hanging over from the weight that I lost and the stretching it had had to do.

'Soon after that I started Pilates and learnt about diastasis recti, muscle separation in the abdomen, which most people have during pregnancy, but usually the muscles close themselves and you're none the wiser. Mine, though, had been so ripped apart by big babies and being unaware of the problem, they didn't recover naturally.

'As I write this now I am recovering from a full tummy tuck. I am happy knowing that I have taken positive action to overcome an issue I was really struggling with, and now I can get on with the rest of my life being confident in my body.'

Restore your core

So, what if you actually despise your shape since having children – maybe you've never quite loved it? Or perhaps you just feel helpless and as if you don't 'know' your body anymore. I'm biased, of course, but Pilates can really be a game changer. Pilates is uniquely positioned to strengthen the muscles that are directly compromised by pregnancy and childbirth: the pelvic floor and abdominals. But if Pilates isn't your bag, any physical activity will help: swimming, yoga, taekwondo – any space you give yourself is time to breathe, to mindfully connect to your body and appreciate its strengths.

Physically strengthening can soften your relationship with your body and begin to release your negative feelings about it. Relaxing your muscles, stretching out toxins, brings more gentle thoughts to the surface. And doing something that tones your body, encourages better body awareness and boosts circulation will also make you feel good.

Notice and retune your internal dialogue (see Chapter 2), and try to find ways of being kinder to yourself. Your body might not be perfect in your eyes – but *no one has a perfect body*. Accept yourself now, as you are; otherwise, however much weight you lose, you may find you're never completely happy with yourself. *You are allowed to love your body.*

You may feel like you're being modest or humbly self-deprecating by constantly berating yourself for your wobbly belly/thunder thighs/childbearing hips, but it's actually weakening your spirit and allowing a negative cloud to linger above your head. Why not try out being completely positive about your body and its unconditional love for you every single day of your life?

Overthink the good. Dwell on the wonderful. Create a positive habit of looking in the mirror every day, smiling, and thinking about at least one part of your body: yes, love it.

Finding flow

Becoming a mother can involve temporarily losing your sense of self, losing sight of the things you like, what makes you 'you', who you are, and what your opinions are about the wider world not related to your children. Connect with your essence, your sense of fun; do some proper belly laughing.

The mythical supermum throws amazing dinner parties and is the life and soul, but she probably also makes time for herself, if she's so damn perfect. So, try to carve out that time if you feel you're missing it. Make sure you have some 'me' time, time to just 'be' and stare out the window, on your own. Try not be a martyr to your life 'shoulds' – there is always time, you might just have to change the way that you use the time that you have.

Put self-care strategies into place as a number-one priority to ensure you're looking after your physical and mental health. Your mental health, and your children, will benefit from you doing anything that allows you find 'flow', a sense of total absorption in the present moment, in the same way as when you were playing as a child. Here are some ideas:

- creative activities, such as writing, blogging, doodling, colouring, puzzles, cooking, pottery, playing or listening to music and crafting
- meeting up with like-minded women to talk about motherhood and its myriad magical challenges, over tea, wine or cocktails
- physical exercise, such as yoga, Pilates, swimming, tai chi, boxing and running
- mindfulness

Eye Movement Desensitisation and Reprocessing (EMDR) is a therapy that uses repetitive movements (eye, hand or body movements), left to right, to aid information processing, to bring relief (see page 10). Swimming lengths of front crawl, drumming, bouncing left to right on a trampoline (hmm, maybe check how robust your pelvic floor is before trying that one) can be soothing and helpful, especially if you are particularly anxious or suffering from a panic attack or PTSD flashback.

The butterfly hug

ACTIVITY

This exercise aims to help you relax more deeply by installing your 'safe place'.

Observe what is happening in your mind throughout this activity, without judging or trying to change it. *Stop when you feel in your body that it has been enough, and lower your hands down.*

- Concentrate on visualising your safe place (see page 77).

- Cross your arms over your chest, so that the tip of the middle finger from each hand is placed below the collarbone, and the other fingers and both hands cover the area under the connection between the collarbone and shoulder and the collarbone and breastbone. Hands and fingers must be as vertical as possible so that the fingers point towards the neck and not towards the arms.

- Interlock your thumbs to form the butterfly's body, and the extension of your other fingers outward will form the butterfly's wings.

- Now close your eyes, or partially close them, and look towards the tip of your nose.

- Move your hands slowly and alternately, like the flapping wings of a butterfly. Let your hands move freely.

- Breathe slowly and deeply (abdominal breathing) while you observe what is going through your mind and body – thoughts, images, sounds, smells, feelings and physical sensations. Picture any images as if they are playing like a film in the cinema.

If you start to feel more anxious or upset by the experience, just stop the exercise, open your eyes and try the grounding techniques described on pages 77 and 156.

'EMDR has been an amazing therapy for my PTSD, much quicker at being effective than chat, which can take years.'
Emma, mum of two and PTSD sufferer

'It was a shock how our lives changed overnight and the strength of emotions which rollercoaster through us on a daily/hourly basis. And the physical challenge after having a c-section. I remember thinking it was like trying to run a marathon with really bad flu.'
Kelly, mum of two

Too much screen time?

Are you aware of spending too much time on your phone while with your children? My dad once showed me a video he had taken (on his phone) when my eldest was a toddler. I was appalled to see in this video that my son was being cuteness personified, and I was in the background glued to my phone, oblivious. It made me feel awful, and I vowed there and then to put the phone down. As much as I can ...

Smartphones are amazing things; they enable us to spend more fun time with our kids by facilitating things that would otherwise require us to spend more boring time away from them – online shopping, organising activities and play dates, keeping up with work from home, etc. But be aware of whether you're scrolling permanently on social media while you're with your child. Put the phone down, be in the present moment.

Social media has myriad influences on your mental state. It can be hugely positive, help to find and create your tribe, give you a high five when you most need it, make you feel like you're not alone, enable you to get multiple opinions on your newborn's poo in the middle of the night. It has broadened friendship horizons for mums in a truly amazing way.

But it can also deplete your confidence if you constantly compare others' final performances to your own life 'behind the scenes', creating the feelings of envy, guilt and sadness that we explored in Chapter 1. Always remember you are *not seeing the full picture* – the tantrums and spilt milk behind the perfect flat lays.

At an Instagram-promoted mothers' event (ironically) it was revealed that smartphones are literally more addictive than heroin.

In order to feel fully present and content, we also need to have some stillness and a clear mind. Too much social media can zap that by becoming a kind of white noise that never switches off – too many things bombarding your internal dialogue like a never-ending news loop across the bottom of your mental screen.

> 'I clung to social media a lot in the first year of motherhood – it seemed like my connection to the outside world (we were then living in a rural area where I knew hardly any other mothers). But now I see that it adds so many pressures on to parenting – your perception of other people's lives and what they present as their lives, compared to how you feel you are doing. Also, comparing your children and their development to other people's presentation of their children. Though, at the same time, it is also nice to see that there are people who are like-minded and parent in a similar way to you, if you feel you haven't come across many in daily life.'
>
> Elizabeth, mum of two

Forming attachment

Antonia Godber, doula, antenatal and baby-massage teacher, educates her new families-to-be about the importance of touch in getting to know your baby.

'Touch is the first of all of the senses to develop – it is fundamental to everything else. Every minute you spend with your baby in your arms, you're helping his brain to grow and develop. Every time you hold him and make eye contact with him and speak to him, you are helping him develop all the social skills he will need for the rest of his life. During those six months, he forms his primary and most secure attachment – to you. After that, he is secure and ready to form bonds with the outside world.'

Your children are now probably well past the newborn cuddling stage. But those early days, when you felt you weren't 'getting anything done' because your baby wouldn't be put down, can contribute to a general low feeling about your competence, which creates a shadow following your mum confidence around. All of those 'empty' moments when you felt like a failure because you sat on the sofa with your baby snoozing on your chest rather than 'getting on with' something – those were moments when you were actually getting the most important stuff 'done': setting the attachment for a healthy loving relationship.

It is never a bad thing for loving touch to feature more prominently in your relationships as this feeds into your attunement to your child (see below) and helps to make you feel *confident* that you're meeting your child's needs. If you've lost sight of your mojo, you have probably also lost sight of how wonderful you are as a mum. Your parenting mojo affects your self-belief and confidence. Focusing on your attunement to your child is a way of bringing back lost sparkle, for you and them.

Attunement and the supermum

The early days of fostering your attachment to your child are imperative in developing your *attunement* to your child. Attunement is being aware of, and responsive to, another person.

So, how does this relate to being (or not being) Supermum? Well, we can become so worried about not being enough, not doing enough, not having enough – not being Supermum – that we sometimes forget to pause and drink in what is right under our noses: our children. Like that cup of tea that we constantly leave to go cold as we're buzzing around doing stuff. Your children, as with your cups of tea, really only need you to focus on them, intently, with love and without distraction.

How does your child feel at the moment – happy, sad, content, anxious? What is the best way to communicate with your child? Is there something you notice in your child's behaviour that is right or wrong – a feeling, an idea? What will engage, encourage and show your child feelings of love and care? Your attunement is very much linked with your *instinct*. In order to get over supermum syndrome, to stop comparing yourself with others and berating yourself for your perceived underachievements, you need to listen to your instincts. Your attunement will be like tuning your radio to the right frequency so that you can hear the messages your instincts are passing to you.

> 'My sons both had dairy allergies when they were babies. I was dismissed by a lot of GPs and health visitors, which made having it diagnosed a much more difficult process than it had to be. It was almost as if they thought I was making it up or not coping! I knew that there was something wrong with my baby – a baby should not be so unsettled and cry in pain so much. It was when I finally saw the paediatrician who said it was a classic case that I knew battling on had been worth it and that my mothering instinct was right.'
>
> Sadie, midwife and mum of two

Attunement has a lot to do with *non-verbal communication*. In fact, most of our communication with our children and others is non-verbal, scarily enough. Maurice often asks me, 'Mummy, why is your face doing that?' if I'm concentrating too hard and frowning when I'm doing his shoelaces or some other mundane task. I wouldn't even be aware that my face looks critical were he not to flag it up for me. (Although in my defence, I do suffer from bitchy resting face; so does Kate Moss – I'm in great company.)

Most of the time we're totally unaware of our non-verbal gestures. But it's kind of like the opposite of a poker face – your feelings will be written all over your face if you're saying something inside. Your child will be able to *sense* your interest in them, as well your approval or disapproval.

If you're generally allowing yourself to be unhappy about yourself, take a quick look to see whether this self-disapproval is coming across in your daily mood, actions and behaviours with your children too. An injection of mummy-mojo will only enhance your relationship with your children. By filling your own cup, you'll be able to pour so much more to others.

Supermum is the perfect mum we compare ourselves to and aspire to be: she may be entirely mythical or we may invest our idea of perfect mumdom into other real women – but rest assured, *all* mothers feel on some level, some days, the lack of mojo that we've been discussing in this chapter. You are not alone. In order for us to sincerely care about others, we also need to give ourselves a bit of love. So if you feel your mojo has gone AWOL, make it a priority to get it back.

5

Lonely yet never alone: how becoming a mum affects your relationships

This chapter will take you through the changing landscape of your relationships since having children. It's completely normal for friendships to fade or disappear, and for family relationships to shift their boundaries – we just need to change how we deal with this if it's leading to unhappiness. We'll refer back to ideas we've explored in Chapter 2 about core beliefs, and see how we can avoid our relationships falling into unnecessary potholes, equipped with a backpack of therapies to help you negotiate the new terrain.

Supermum is at the centre of her (Pinterest-worthy, natch) home, the hub of all things warm and nurturing, cooking nourishing meals at her Aga for her adoring close and extended family. She has a 'girl gang', a solid close network of friendships – she's an alpha friend, daughter, daughter-in-law, sister. Her relationship with her partner also brings its A-game at all times, and is enviable for its chemistry ... The reality of motherhood is that relationships can often fall far, far short of this supermum ideal.

The connections in your spider's web of life-relationships take on a different dynamic, have different parameters, seek different reassurances after you've have children. Sometimes this is momentary turbulence. You may have settled into an equilibrium quite soon with your nearest and dearest, once you'd got the hang of leaving the house with nappies and sanity packed.

You might have negotiated mum-and-baby-group territory effortlessly, and have emerged with lifelong mum friends to get through crappy days drinking prosecco happily with. But, often, the dynamic shift is more permanent, and without an understanding of the whys and wherefores allowing you to navigate your way into accepting a new relationship landscape, you're left feeling like you're quite alone, but never on your own.

As we saw in Chapter 1, the heightened emotions that motherhood brings – frustration, anger, hate, guilt – surface because the notion of intimacy takes on a whole new level once you bring the chaos and messiness of child birth and rearing into the equation. Your personal space is somehow stretched like a surrealist painting: some relationships uninvitedly become terrifyingly intense, and others are suddenly pushed far into the distance while you can only look on, softly calling 'come back, come back'.

The social isolation of being a new mum

As soon as you become pregnant, attitudes shift around you. By stealth, dynamics change as your bump evolves: at work, in the pub, with your in-laws. Questions become strangely more intrusive, childless friends may begin to back off; there's a kind of limbo between being childless and being a mother.

This feeling of isolation continues once your baby arrives: sheer logistics of getting out of the house to see people, heightened levels of anxiety, simply not knowing anyone in a similar boat to hang out with. Add to that the loss of identity that we explored in Chapter 4, and our relationships can really take a battering.

'I feel like I don't have a brain to have a coherent conversation about anything interesting, so always end up feeling like a lame person with no chat, when I meet mums at toddler groups. It makes me feel really useless. I crave being with a group of old friends who know me, but none of my old friends are in the same situation. I definitely feel like I don't know who I am, and my social life is the thing that has died as a result.'

Leah, mum of one

Even if you have a reliable troop of friends, those first few months as a mum can be overwhelming in its loneliness. In 2016, Channel 4 News produced a programme about the social isolation and loneliness of new mums, exposing a toxic mix of exhaustion, self-doubt and simply not having the energy to create the social networks needed to soften the blow.

A survey published by the *Daily Mail* in 2013 suggested that 55% of new mums missed their social life more than anything else from their childless life. An interesting nugget from the survey was that new mums wished they had known that 'mums in the same position may have only been appearing to cope'. Hello, Supermums – it's hard to break out of the cycle and be honest about feeling like crap when you think that everyone else is in a supermum club that you're not invited to. Actually, it's simply that no one is admitting *there is no supermum club.*

'Two babies in, I feel like I'm now consuming all the happiness and precious moments I missed in those first six months of my first baby. I'm happy, content and surrounded by people, friends, who are finally just like me. I wish my current self could revisit the new-mum me and tell her to chill the f*ck out, everything would turn out OK. People didn't lie or dupe me into believing motherhood was a good thing, it IS a good, amazing, thing, I just had a really shitty, tough first few months – and when you haven't been through that before, you have no idea that doesn't last forever. But it doesn't, and it changes pretty fast and then it's really easy to forget how bloody lonely and hard and anxiety-inducing it can be. I think mums forget that really easily, and I think, as a society, we need to remember how

*lonely and sacrificial becoming a mother can feel when you've
never done it before.'*

Amy, mum of two

Motherhood binds us, but can also separate us: we're all mothers, but
of course that doesn't necessarily mean we're all the same and will
automatically get on like a house on fire. We need to build like-minded
networks and forge connections.

The transient nature of mothering phases – babydom, nursery,
preschool, big school and beyond – and the energies needed to be
devoted to keeping all the general plates spinning, can keep us stuck in
social isolation. Most of us don't realise, pre-baby, that we'll need to put
quite a lot of effort into making new friends that fit with these 'phases',
and that long-term connections may take a while to settle.

Loneliness taps into your core beliefs

If, after the initial mayhem of the toddler tunnel – let's face it, it's
impossible to maintain a conversation while perpetually chasing after
a small person – you still feel lonely and that you haven't slotted into a
supportive network of friendships, it's worth finding strategies to
understand how you can get around this.

Loneliness, or the social anxiety that stems from seeking new friends,
can sometimes reignite core beliefs that were bobbing along
unobtrusively pre-children – believing you are unlikeable or unpopular,
for example. So, without realising it, you may be looking for evidence
that you're Norma No Mates, and are thereby hindering any efforts
that people might be making to reach out to you.

CBT techniques can be useful in these circumstances. Rather than
attaching your loneliness or lack of social life to *you* and your
characteristics or qualities, unhook it from yourself and attach it to
your *circumstances*. This may be a *lonely period of time* in your life, but
it is not a fixed circumstance and it will end. Come back to noticing
your internal dialogue in order to become aware if you're falling victim
to self-sabotage.

Affirmations – shifting the cycle, looking for positive evidence

Overcoming loneliness may involve finding simple strategies to help you get around social anxiety and allow you to connect to people comfortably once more. Positive self-talk can provide very useful affirmations to being your own cheerleader when you most need a boost.

Here are some examples for:

1. **preparing,** i.e. before you are entering a situation that may cause you some anxiety – a school party, for example
2. **coping** while you're in the situation – this is the pep talk in the loos
3. **praising/reviewing** – giving yourself a high five when you've got through it.

Preparing

- `It's not going to be as bad as you think.'
- `It's better to go than not to go. Worry doesn't help.'
- `If I do get bad feelings, I know they won't last long and I can deal with them.'
- `I do not need to compare myself to others.'
- `Today I will see the best in myself and my child.'

Coping

- `Take one step at a time.'
- `I know I am going to be OK.'
- `Remember to relax and think positive.'

Praising/Reviewing

- `I did that well.'
- `I handled that – it'll be easier next time.'
- `I accept and embrace my imperfections.'
- `I release fear, doubt and guilt.'

- `I'm confident in my decisions.'
- `Every day I learn and grow as a mother.'

Try to create some affirmations for yourself as well.

The above sentences are short and simple, but write them down (along with your own affirmations), commit to saying them to yourself out loud if you can, and you really will begin to overturn your negative internal thought processes.

Best Friends Forever ...?

How does Supermum have so many close friends while I feel like I'm at the periphery of many friend groups but at the centre of none? Is it normal for relationships to change once we become mums?

We have to realise that *it's OK to let things change* at this stage of your life, when you need different things from different relationships. They ebb and flow according to circumstance, and one closing door may lead to doors opening into another corridor.

The saying goes, 'Make new friends, but keep the old, one is silver and the other gold.' So what happens when you feel like you've been robbed of both silver and gold, and you're left with scraps of tin and copper?

> *'I am a different person since having kids. I used to go out all the time; now I hardly ever do. I used to be ambitious; now I'm pleased if I manage to leave the house wearing matching socks. I used to go to the cinema, art galleries, theatre, and have lots to say about culture ... now my favourite topic of conversation is the best playgrounds or schools in the area. I'm dull.'*
>
> Tina, mum of three

> *'I feel like I doubt myself socially now more ... If I do go out without my children I feel anxious that I don't have a "buffer", I'm kind of naked without them running around me, without an obvious given conversation point, or a "way out" if I'm struggling with conversation.'*
>
> Belinda, mum of two

I have dear lovely friends I now don't see very often, and, as the months stretch into years, I'm forced to admit that some friendship has faded into the past through no fault of, well ... anyone's. The logistics of keeping the embers burning of that friendship were clearly beyond what either of us were happy to breathe into it, but I can gaze back fondly at the relationship. Life pushes people in different directions, and sometimes a friendship will have to be left, like a passenger at a particular interchange, as your bus continues to chug along on its road.

You might lose friends due to the logistics of motherhood – no time, no money, no babysitting, no brain – or even due to your motherhood choices bringing you apart from friends who suddenly seem judgemental, or who you can't help but judge for their choices. Any friendship loss can feel painful, almost like a divorce. You might feel confused, hurt and unsure of how to move forward with other friendships under this surrounding veil of unease and insecurity.

Sadly, this is part of parenthood, and indeed life. We all evolve, and like the waxing and waning moon there are changing seasons and we have to learn to flow with them. When someone exits your life, chances are there is someone else who will emerge into this phase of it. But also think of life as a continuously changing and regenerating thing; nothing is ever fixed. A door may close. But it's a door: it can open again – that's what doors do.

Fertility and friendship

Having children can put a whole new emotional stake on a friendship, stronger than any rivalry or jealousy experienced before. Nothing shows the unfairness of life more than the fertility lottery. The arrival of children can make this more cruelly obvious if your friends are popping out babies left, right and centre, and you're not childless by choice.

> 'Some of us would love to have children but can't. I've had three unsuccessful cycles of IVF, and however much I want and try to be completely happy for my friends when they have children, it's always going to be difficult. Seeing their baby pics will always feel like a heartbreak and remind me of what I can't have. I

> *make them feel guilty, they make me feel sad. It's a major threat*
> *to friendship and sometimes it just feels too hard. These days I*
> *just feel more comfortable with childless friends.'*

Kath

Have you had friendships that fizzled out around the baby-making time and you weren't sure why? Sometimes you never really know what people are going through until years after the event. It may be that while you were happily procreating, your friend was struggling, be it with infertility or miscarriage – both of which are usually swathed in silent taboo – and not able to connect to you as a result.

My best friend and I navigated the choppy journey of fertility issues, rocking a friendship boat that had otherwise sailed happily for 15 years. She had been trying for a baby for three years and was just about to embark on her first round of IVF when I told her I was pregnant. I was the last in a long line of friends who had recently told her that 'happy' news, and she simply couldn't cope and so cut me off.

While I struggled with early motherhood, she was the person I wanted to confide in. She, heartbrokenly childless and (she thought) facing a future without children, couldn't entertain the idea that becoming a mother was anything but joyful. After a couple of unsuccessful attempts to reach out, I didn't want to feel like I was rubbing her nose in anything, so the silence prevailed.

As often does, fortunes flipped in the next couple of years and she happily got pregnant, first by IVF and then again naturally, while I went on to have several miscarriages. Thankfully, we were ultimately determined to remain friends and so made sure that we kept the lines of communication open, forced ourselves into a few tricky conversations that we could easily have shied away from, and we have emerged just as strong.

It goes to show that, although sometimes it may be *easier* to let a relationship go, a little bit of hard, honest graft can keep it afloat, and you won't regret putting in that effort. Friendships *can* survive change, but you need to be prepared to give them a helping hand: imagine a friendship is like a garden – you need to get on your knees, do some weeding, digging, nurture the soil and plant new seeds.

Losing old friends

Friendship loss can be a fairly taboo subject, and yet the loss of a female friendship can be every bit as intense as the breakup of a relationship. There are many reasons for friendship breakups, shifts and changes. Having children is one of them that many of us can relate to. Losing a beloved friend brings with it a heady mixture of pain, confusion and a sense of deep loss.

I *want* to be as good a friend as ever, but it's just not possible. I don't think I'm alone in this struggle. Many mums I spoke to talked about feeling very thinly spread between their home/work life and their friendships, and it's always the friendship that is sacrificed.

> 'It's easy to feel that everything in your own life is perceived as trivial and meaningless, or even hedonistic, compared to family life. And as much as I try, I can't really be that interested in child-related problems as I just don't have any valuable advice to give. So I've drifted away from a lot of old friendships as a result.'
>
> Natasha

An old school friend and ex-flatmate, childless, sent me a long email the other day out of the blue and at the end asked me, 'What have you been up to?' ... I sighed inwardly, thinking of the two trips to A&E I'd had with my eldest in the past month, and the ongoing separation anxiety and sleeplessness from my toddler, and thought ... ergh I don't know how to reply adequately in a way that would be interesting to her. And then I forgot to reply as I have a goldfish memory for non-'essential' things. When I do meet up, childless friends probably don't quite appreciate the military effort it takes for me to turn up late, have nothing interesting to say, and go home early.

Give and take

Established friendships inevitably change when you become a mother as your priorities and your time pressures shift, but you can feel aggrieved if they change without you being able to control it, and they start to slip beyond your grasp. Given the supermum image of alpha friend, you might feel you're failing if you don't have a supportive set of close friends around you, having your back at all times – or simply feel annoyed that your friends aren't supporting you or keeping in touch enough, in your view.

> 'Finding the time and energy to be a wife as well as a friend and a mother causes me to become anxious and stressed – it's very easy for me to feel like I'm failing someone, and that's hard to digest.'
>
> Sarah-Jane, mum and stepmum of two

If a friendship feels unequal, with one of you making all the effort, that's when resentment can start to fester. Whether it's you making all the effort, or if you can sense that gradually friends have stopped reaching out, sadly this is a natural thing that happens. Rather than letting resentment set in, take a moment to wonder what factors might be at play.

Check whether you're listening to *facts* in your thought dialogue, or whether your automatic thoughts are making the situation look different. Consider the friendship from the other side. We all tend to think that our way is the 'right' way. It's sometimes useful to stand in someone else's shoes, to have a sense of what they might be feeling, thinking and experiencing. In their shoes, what do they think about you and how you have behaved? What would they like to say to you, and how are they feeling?

Try to open up a dialogue rather than spend futile energy festering. See friendship as an organic being: it can change and morph, maybe hibernate, and come back to life after winter.

> 'As an "unchild" person, even if you try to maintain the friendship, the parent will rarely confide in you because you "won't understand".'
>
> Suki

Losing a friendship is hardly ever just *one* person's fault. If you've been brave enough to end a friendship because it wasn't healthy and was making you feel crap, the end of that relationship most certainly *isn't* your fault. Try not to beat yourself up over friendships ending, for not being able to keep someone in your life. It really is OK to let some go, like balloons into the sky.

You'll hopefully continue to have friends that you've known and loved since always, and with whom you'll probably still be friends when you're old and grey. But not all friendships are meant to last forever. Some very worthwhile, meaningful friendships can come into your life just for a brief period, and that's life.

Rummage through your friend closet

ACTIVITY

This activity will help you to evaluate your various friendships in more detail.

- Think of your friendship groups as a wardrobe.
- Visualise the different 'outfits' that you need.
- Consider each of your friends as a piece of clothing, to put on when you most need it.
- Think about the seasons: what kinds of situation require what types of friend?
- Note down which of your friends are staples: a classic coat to support you through all weathers, a great black dress, a killer pair of heels, the comfy jeans you wear all the time so they've moulded to your shape.
- Others may be fashion items that you only wear once in a blue moon – you feel amazing when you do, but they're just not practical for day-to-day wear.
- Maybe others at the back of your wardrobe haven't been worn for a while, but actually you should dust them off and try them on again.
- And think about which ones no longer spark joy, or don't fit any more, and perhaps consider sending them to the charity shop.

Doing a friendship 'audit' like this occasionally will encourage you to understand not only what your friendships bring to you, but what you offer them as well. It's never too late to attempt to re-establish contact with someone you haven't been in touch with for a while. And, similarly, it can be healthy to recognise when a relationship has run its course.

This activity might help you to uncover that not all friendships will be soulmate-level friendships – we all have different 'tiers' to our friendship auditorium, with each bringing a different quality to our lives. This is to be expected, and is entirely positive and normal.

Maybe you have friends who are almost more like work colleagues: mums that you hang out with to pass the time and see most days – more than you see your close friends – but who you might not completely click with on a deeper level, or share world views with.

The supermum mum-friend myth

Finding your tribe, desperately seeking your girl gang: acquiring plenty of acquaintances among the parents of your children's friends is a breeze, but real, lasting 'mum-friendship' can be much trickier.

Learning how to make new 'mum friends' is a bit like re-entering the dating game you might have left behind a long time ago, only without the happy-hour drinks. The etiquette of asking for someone's number, the worry about appearing too eager if you ask someone to meet you for a coffee after the school run – the 'what if she's just not that into me?' – or, she's your mum crush but your kids just don't get on so it's awkward: it's all a potential social-anxiety minefield.

> 'It will just happen. I didn't make friends with an antenatal class or at toddler groups, but once my first son started preschool I made loads, without forcing it. It is difficult, just because you both have children it doesn't mean to you have enough in common to sustain a friendship, and it's so hard getting past the small talk when you have a toddler running amok. Once they start school and make their own friends, it definitely becomes easier for you too.'
>
> Kate, mum of three

A lot of mums said to me that they felt the first few years of mum-friendship forays could leave them feeling a bit 'irked' – slightly bruised or judged by other mums, feeling like the environment wasn't as safe or likeminded as you'd hoped it would be. Sharing motherhood experiences without feeling scrutinised for your choices apparently isn't as easy as it could be. Many mums mentioned 'cliquey playgroup mums', being 'left out' and feeling like you're not 'in the crew'.

> 'Lack of confidence has been a huge challenge for me – as a young mother I felt embarrassed for the first year or so after my son was born. All the mothers I met were about ten years older than me and I felt like they were confused by my choice to have a baby in my early twenties. When I was pregnant and went to a meeting of local pregnant mothers I got asked by a mother, "Oh, so was it a mistake?" and I think that really affected me. It took me a while to feel confident in myself, publicly, as a mother.'
>
> Elizabeth, mum of two

Mum friends are important, yes, but they will come when they come – returning to the garden metaphor, you can't rush those green shoots. A bit like the friends you make at Freshers' Week at university – it may be that the mates who are in it for the long haul are the ones you find once you're feeling more confident in your footing, rather than those you cling to in the early stages.

Try not to put up unnecessary barriers, or write things off too soon. We're all muddling along juggling our priorities, so continue reaching out and you never know what might follow from it. Try to be at peace with the fact that some relationships are more transient than others – motherhood 'phases' can bring this more acutely to the fore.

> 'I found it so hard to "break into" mum groups. I'm definitely not shy, but it's difficult to move in on "ready-made" groups and easy to feel rejected. I went to a toddler group and looked out for a friendly looking group of mums. Went and asked if I could join them and they said yes. Still felt a bit left out for a few weeks because they'd all known each other from NCT and met up outside of the playgroup. So every week I sat with them, listened, laughed at their jokes, picked up on things they said and asked questions. Eventually I became accepted. But it took time.'
>
> Eleanor, mum of two

Competitive-mum syndrome

When you already feel inadequate, innocent questions such as 'Is she sleeping through the night?', or 'Does he do after-school art club?', can feel like hot prongs searing into the fragile snowman of your self-esteem. Suddenly you're immediately concerned about your child *not* sleeping, or being at after-school art club. Should they be? Shit, I'm a crap mum. When you're muddling your way through, you assume supermum self-confidence in the know-all mother asking you these questions.

'Comparison – comparing myself and/or my child to others' is a killer. It shakes your confidence, makes you question your outlook, causes you to become an unnecessary judge and feel a little depleted. I quickly learnt to try not to judge others or myself. All mums and all babies are different; with differing needs, differing approaches and the only thing that should matter is finding what works for us.'

Sarah-Jane, mum and stepmum of two

In actual fact, when another mum asks you questions about your child's development that you feel are judgemental or intrusive, chances are she's just seeking reassurance about the way that she's doing things herself. So we all need to take a moment, and not be too quick to judge other mums, or make the mistake of interpreting other mothers' parenting choices, or even thoughtless quip, as a slight or condemnation of our own.

'It is really important to surround yourself with women you can be completely, completely yourself with. As we get older our experience gives us the confidence we want and need. We learn to surround ourselves with women who lift and build you up, and are strong enough to (politely) ignore those who don't.'

Antonia, antenatal teacher and mum of three

'Competitive mothers are insecure. If they have the time or need to compare your mothering skills with their own – or worse still, your baby with theirs – it's because they're unsure, not because they're mean. Still, it doesn't mean that you have to hang around with them.'

Kathryn, mum of two

Clashing parenting styles

Even old friendships that have weathered many storms can come unstuck if you have very different parenting styles, which can simply affect you all being able to hang out without awkwardness. Areas of etiquette that you didn't have to confront before kids suddenly rear their heads: you might allow your child to jump down from the table as soon as they're done, but your friend adamantly wants theirs to stay while everyone else finishes their meal.

Rules around eating times, allowed foods, watching TV, whether toddlers drink from sippy cups or bottles, crying it out, not to mention the can of worms that is approaches to discipline, can all cause tension between friends where previously things were relatively easy-going and revolved mainly around who's paying for the next round. Parenthood makes us opinionated. This is fact, and quite a positive thing generally, but it can make for awkward conversations if friendship and parenting ethos clashes.

It can be a bitter pill to swallow to feel judged by close friends, or even just by acquaintances, when it's clear that your parenting styles diverge. You have to make a decision about either pushing your point of view, and potentially causing offence, or staying silent and maintaining peace. Having your child told off by someone else, for something you may not have thought was too serious, is particularly challenging – as is when you feel your friend really shouldn't let some behaviour slide.

But, as with many of the tricky scenarios we have encountered so far, it's always worth taking a deep breath and acknowledging that there are two sides to every story. If your friendship is strong enough, it can withstand these issues without losing affection and intimacy. And if not, it's time to allow it to loosen anyway.

> '*I feel mortified when my child goes up to the host and demands the party bag as soon as we arrive at a party. The shame of it always makes me wish the ground would swallow me up.*'
>
> Annie, mum of two

'Whenever I have a friend around and their child starts kicking
off and being a complete nightmare, it's actually quite
reassuring. It's nice to know it's not just me who has to deal with
that kind of thing, as sometimes that's how it feels: that you're a
total shambles and everyone else has it together.'

Lucy, mum of two

Your mother and other close family members

Families. You can choose your friends, but you can't choose your family. The birth of a baby may bring some relationships with family closer than you expect (hello, trying to breastfeed in front of your father-in-law), and others may become more distant or challenging. It is perhaps obvious, but only when we have our own children do we fully realise the influence our own parents had on how we 'turned out'.

There are unspoken judgements and rules for supermums that, as we're gradually breaking down through this book, are unattainable in real life – maybe there are rules that we think grandparents, aunties and uncles and the wider family 'should' abide by. If you feel you're not being offered the support you expect, or you feel boundaries are being crossed – open up a dialogue about it with those concerned, or make notes for yourself in your notebook to assemble what exactly is causing you stress, rather than stewing.

Everyone's situation is different – some mums feel that their own mothers are taking over when grandchildren come into the mix; whereas others resent the fact their mothers don't help them more. It's best to be clear about the kind of help you want, rather than going along with what's offered and feeling resentful.

Family (and friends, and strangers on the bus ...) will inevitably offer advice and opinions about your parenting – sometimes unasked for and sometimes in conflict with your own ideas – and occasionally it makes you want to drive your face into the nearest wall. If you disagree with the advice being offered, it can help to focus on the fact that it is usually well meaning, and that it's up to you to decide whether to take on board the advice given or just nod and say 'mm hmmm' non-specifically and move on.

Your relationship with your own mum

Becoming a mother inevitably brings under close scrutiny our own experience as a child, our relationship with our own mother, or if you've lost or are estranged from your mother it brings that loss acutely to the fore. The way you were parented informs your parenting, whether or not you're fully conscious of that. You may be keen to 'make up for' any mistakes you felt your own mother made, and aim for supermum perfection as a way of redemption for what you felt you suffered when you were a child.

> 'All my life I struggled with the feeling that my mum just didn't understand me. Now that I'm a mother, I realise that I never understood HER. It never occurred to me that my mother was a person, a woman. She navigated the tricky waters of raising two children, trying to teach me to be independent, responsible, confident, while also grappling with how to be a good wife, a good mother, a good friend herself.'
>
> Emily, mum of two

The good-enough mother

The psychologist D. W. Winnicott presented the concept of the 'good enough mother' in 1953, outlining how it's important that a child sees that their mother is ultimately fallible and not perfect. In fact, it is an imperfect mother who will raise her child more effectively. Mums should be (and I'm paraphrasing here) farmers rather than goddesses: intuitively responding to our children and the circumstances we are in at that moment, and learning from our mistakes rather than feeling that no mistakes should ever be made.

> 'The good-enough mother ... starts off with an almost complete adaptation to her infant's needs, and as time proceeds she adapts less and less completely, gradually, according to the infant's growing ability to deal with her failure.'
>
> D. W. Winnicott

Sadly this perceived imperfection and 'failure' can cut deep sometimes, as Vicky, a mum of one, illustrates: 'Before I became a mum my vision of motherhood was that I wanted to be the opposite of everything my mother did for me. I wanted him to be loved, to be accepting and kind to others. I would make all of his meals myself and ensure he never watched too much TV and had everything I never had. He would want for nothing, and always know how proud I am of him.'

Sophie, a mum of two, has always had a strained relationship with her mum. 'I actually have found that the only way to deal with it is to expect nothing from her: no emotional support, no logistical support, no care, no connection. She is in her own little world and it's only after my second child was born and she didn't even meet him until he was six months old – she lives about an hour away – that I fully realised how little she prioritises me. So now I expect nothing, and if there is anything from her then that's a bonus.'

Your relationship with your mother (or the primary caregiver if your mum wasn't around), and particularly the earliest years of attachment forming, is what lays the bricks in place for the foundation of your core beliefs. It is this early, pre-verbal attunement (see pages 118–120) and connection that first teaches you whether you are loved and valued, whether relationships are secure and to be trusted – or whether you feel undervalued and unsupported.

If your mother was unable to give you that early nurturing, this can be a difficult thing to come to terms with. There is something powerful about realising that your mother did not give you a great start in life. Babies and children internalise everything – abused children can develop core beliefs such as 'I am a bad person' and 'There is something wrong with me.' Neglected children can believe, 'I am unlovable' or 'I am unimportant.'

We can carry internalised messages from the way our parents were with us as core beliefs without even realising it. Children often accept or interpret responsibility ('I deserved it'/'I caused it'/'I wasn't good enough'/'I wasn't lovable enough'/'It was my fault – there's something wrong with me') without questioning. Knowing that 'bad things happen to good people' can often be a revelation for adults who had toxic childhoods.

If you have never given time to doing this, think back on your own childhood, and particularly your relationship with your own mother. What messages might you have internalised from the way she was with you? If you recognise negative core beliefs in yourself then try to make links about where these have come from. If you have difficult memories that stand out, ask yourself what you think each memory says about you. Common beliefs might include, 'I am weak', 'I am bad' or 'I am worthless.'

If we have had difficult childhoods, we often hold difficult memories at the age and stage at which they happened. This can account for why certain memories can still cause us to feel, think and behave as we were when we were children. We are still experiencing them as children, not as our 30- or 40-odd-year-old adult selves.

A pivotal change before making a decision to give your children a better 'mother' has to involve 'mothering yourself'. It is OK to grieve for that mother that you didn't have. Think of ways that you can nurture yourself now, and keep a check on your self-berating if you feel you are not 'perfect' enough. Good enough is good enough.

Turning into your mother

It might be that you want to emulate your mum but feel that you can never live up to how wonderful she is/was. Emma, a mum of two, says, 'I'm always "out-mummed" by my own mother ... she's got parenting licked. She's wonderful, but a hard role model to live up to. She had four easy home births so I felt like a failure compared to her with my two car crashes. Being a mum was like her calling in life. She was at home with us and just was the best mum in the world. I always feel like I can never be as good a mother as she is and make it look as easy as she did.'

If you feel you're mothering in the shadow of your mother's unattainable greatness, try to look at your own achievements objectively and kindly, rather than with critical glasses on. Remember that it's how you make your children *feel* rather than what you *do* that is the most important thing, ultimately. If your mum made it look easy, it doesn't mean it was, you just didn't see her hard work – in the same way that your kids probably don't see yours.

Try to step back and see the bigger picture regarding the way your mum parented. Ask yourself, 'What enabled my mum to be so emotionally available?' She may have been able to stay home whereas you work; had fewer financial difficulties than those you face; have family close by. Often we can view how our parents parented through children's eyes – looking at the whole situation as an adult may open new understandings about the differences between your mum's situation and your own.

Also remember that most coherent memories are most likely to be over the age of four – so we are unlikely to remember much before then that isn't a range of body sensations or emotions that we can struggle to make sense of. So, this again colours how we see our parents.

> 'I pretty much thought I'd be like my mum, with a few tweaks – I knew it would be important to make time for my partner and for myself ... what I didn't know was how difficult this would be to put into practice (I became a Velcro Mum with an edge of Mama Guilt).'
>
> Sarah-Jane, mum and stepmum of two

A lot of mums told me that since becoming a mum they have felt huge guilt for what a monster they were to their mum when they were a teenager. If you're feeling guilty, be reassured that, well, teenagers are officially a bit crazy. Sarah-Jayne Blakemore is a leading social neuroscientist of adolescent development. In 2014 she opened a discussion about the fact that teenagers' brains are still forming. It's natural and to be expected – even encouraged – that they therefore need to thrash around and push against the status quo a bit, to challenge boundaries, to break from their tethers and forge their own identities away from their mums. So, I'm sure your mum will graciously accept a belated apology for monster teenage times. And, well, karma. Your children will no doubt do the same to you.

Mothering without your own mother

Sarah Turner, *The Unmumsy Mum* author and blogger, lost her mum when she was a child. In her first book she dedicates a chapter to her mum: 'You were – and still are – my parenting idol. You are the closest thing I've ever known to a real Supermum, and I'm so proud that the real Supermum was *my mum* ... being a mum without a mum is just so bloody unfair.'

When you've lost your mum, it can feel profoundly like she is present everywhere in her absence, and it makes the loss feel all the more great when you hear other people talking about how much they do with granny, or simply moaning about their mums.

The traditional grief narrative asks you to say goodbye to loved ones, and to 'move on' in your life without them, accept the permanence of the loss. The psychologist Michael White turned this around with his 'Saying hullo again' article, in which he invites people to try to reclaim the relationship they had with their lost loved one. Instead of closing a door on that person and the relationship you shared, open up a dialogue and, simply, say hello again. He asks the following questions.

- *What did your mother see, when she looked at you through her loving eyes?*
- *How did she know these things about you?*
- *What is it about you that told her this?*
- *What difference would it make to how you feel if you carried this knowledge with you in daily life?*

Michael White

The aim of these questions is to acknowledge the importance of the person in your life (still), and to strengthen the connection between you and them.

When we become mothers, we become all too aware of how human and inadequate we are. If we can transfer some of this insight to our own mothers, this can help us see them in different ways.

We can become separated from our mothers for many reasons. Some of these separations are necessary. Some mother–daughter relationships are so toxic that, for our own good, distance can be helpful. If you are estranged from your mother, scan your body to see if this brings up any strong emotions. If so, question why. Your emotions may be prompting you to act – to make contact again, or to distance yourself further – or to help you validate your current situation and finally find some peace.

Mother-in-law dynamics

Pressure from mothers, partners and mothers-in-law can undermine your self-confidence and breed self-doubt. The mother-in-law relationship can be particularly tricky, as you're less likely to feel able to set your own parameters. Therefore you may feel out of control with the emotional equation between the two of you, particularly if it comes down to your partner 'siding' with one of you over the other, or not supporting you when you clash. You may feel like suddenly you've 'disappeared' and aren't important, now that you've provided grandchildren. You may feel questioned and challenged, constantly. Or maybe you feel that she's *too* hands off.

> '*I wasn't overly keen on visitors or accepting help from my mother-in-law as I often felt she was intrusive, critical and unsupportive. I felt guilty for feeling like this, but also allowed myself time. I have a hard time differentiating between interference and help – I easily feel criticised and can become incredibly defensive, which in turn makes me anxious about certain social situations with my children.*'
>
> Sarah-Jane, mum and stepmum of two

One useful thing to remember is that, if you're a mum of boys, chances are that one day *you* will be in this mother-in-law position if your son has children. See if this alters your perception of your grievances. When things are tough, know that it is a changing landscape; it doesn't have to be that way permanently – all relationships can grow and change, if given the chance.

With my first baby I was hypersensitive to what I perceived as my mother-in-law's judgement and criticism of my 'failed' birth and subsequent struggle to breastfeed (heightened anxiety due to my bad birth experience definitely didn't help regulate my reactions). She is a home-birthing/breastfeeding guru and I felt like a failure in the light of that.

Looking back, we were both working our way around establishing the parameters of a new relationship. It was much smoother second time round – I was more resilient, she was softer in her approach. Basically, we had settled more comfortably into the mother/grandmother roles.

If you find that you are stuck in an unhelpful rut with relations with your mother-in-law, see how you can make it easier for yourself by trying the calming and grounding activity on page 77 to lessen your anxiety. Or, simply, detach yourself emotionally a bit using the activity that follows, so as not to feel so uncomfortably embroiled.

Exclusive club membership

ACTIVITY

Imagine that your life is an exclusive club and you can choose what level of pass you give to members.

Write down the people in your life and decide on the level of access that they're granted. For example:

- your mother-in-law only gets weekend membership
- some people have off-peak access only
- your best friend has a GOLD anytime pass.

By writing down the level of involvement you are allowing certain people in your life, you can distance yourself from the impact their behaviour is having on you.

Family dynamics

Your relationships also extend to your children – you may not really observe your 'relationship' with your children but instead just let it be, day to day. But it's worth sometimes reflecting on how you all interact, and getting a feel for the family dynamics that are being set up, which will probably be entrenched in your Christmases forever.

Family therapy works around the concept of the family as a 'living system' – within which each part has a knock-on effect on each other. The least happy member is merely the one expressing dissatisfaction on behalf of the whole family, or the one highlighting what is a whole-family issue.

Difficulties are never present within just one member of the family, but in the 'relationship space' in between. If you think that one of your children is the lone source of your whole family's problems, you simply need to widen your lens. This child is often really important because they are highlighting a bigger issue that you are missing.

Challenges – those soul-destroying fights and miscommunications that happen every day – highlight all sorts of rules and principles about how families run, which you might need to give some thought to (and possibly revise). Even if they don't seem it, children are the least powerful members of any family system, *so it is always up to us as parents to make changes.*

Be honest with yourself. If you have more than one child, do you have a favourite? Do you always interact in the same way with each child? Have you got into habits without realising it? Do you label your children within their earshot: 'he's so bossy', 'he's always a nightmare at bedtime', 'she's the grumpy one'? Have a look at your family dynamic and notice the ways that this might manifest itself and inform the atmosphere within the family.

Look also at your own family: your relationship with your parents, your siblings. Do you always react defensively when your mum comments about certain things in a certain way? Are those reactions set in concrete, mired in years of history and buried under layers of family narrative 'truth'? Perhaps you are 'the distant one', while your little sister is 'the baby of the family' who curries your parents' favour in a really annoying way. Could you pause and decide to change the way you view your relationships – see your dynamic as something new, moving and reactive rather than set in stone?

If you can see the longer-term patterns that are created by daily interactions and small acts of unforgiveness, you can begin to see your own family settling a different track, like footprints in new snow. Snow may fall and cover these footprints – they don't have to be fixed and set there irrevocably.

Your family is only as happy as the least happy member of the family, so they say. Who might be the least happy member, and why? Take some time in your notebook to observe some wonderful qualities about your children, and notice details about their relationship with each other/with the wider family. View them through loving eyes.

Your relationship with your partner

Supermum might have a fun, sexy, intimate relationship with her partner for life, but Good-Enough Mum sometimes feels as if there is unreasonable pressure to be a perfect partner when motherhood is draining her of emotional and physical resources. The change from a couple to a family of three (or more if twins were your first), is one of the biggest transformations you face when you become a parent. Some couples grow stronger as they find a new respect for each other as parents, a swell of love that carries them through any stormy waters.

There is a real balance shift: before babies you had an equal footing of two people against the world, and this altered forever once your little passenger disembarked. Your partner suddenly becomes your co-pilot, and occasionally you start to rely on autopilot rather than seeing each other as the new, interesting, enticing person you once knew. Sleep deprivation only saturates it. You're so busy and tired that you forget to show your adoration or even liking for each other. Without signs of appreciation, misunderstanding can creep in.

Make sure you don't just say what you're unhappy with, constantly. Share the good stuff too. The magic ratio is 5:1 – as long as there are five times as many positive interactions between partners as there are negative, the relationship is likely to be happy and stable.

Decisions about parenting after childbirth

One of the most difficult things to manage with your relationship as parents is if you have differing views on how to parent – one of you might be an all-night family-bed cuddler, and the other a staunch Gina Ford devotee, and this can cause real conflict. It can be easy for one parent to become the 'expert' and undermine the other's confidence.

> 'Every now and again I have a blip day and become upset that my husband doesn't think I am the "best". His opinion matters to me and I want him to think I am Supermum … regardless of how unrealistic and unobtainable that may be. It's just that I want him to be proud of me for mothering his children. If I've managed to go through a day without arguing with him due to

> *parenting "differences", and have not been completely*
> *depleted of mental energy, it has been a successful one.'*
> Sarah-Jane, mum and stepmum of two

It helps to discuss each other's views and try to develop a joint approach, and accepting that you may have different ways of looking after your children is really important – just because you do things differently doesn't mean that one way is right or wrong (however strongly you feel about the way your partner packs the changing bag).

Encourage your partner's independent relationship with your child: supermum syndrome can mean trying to take it all on yourself, to the detriment of this relationship. It's hard to let go, to relinquish control and, possibly, expose yourself to your fears of your partner finding their own way and, shock horror, maybe even doing it better.

Show your faith, give them the reins, delegate the responsibility, and this will boost their relationship with your children. And also, as a pleasant side-effect, it'll allow you some space and freedom to be you – checking back in on your mojo, as we saw in the previous chapter – which will ultimately allow you to be a better mum.

'Fun dad' syndrome – differences in discipline

Nothing is more annoying than when you feel undermined because of something your partner does that in an instant overturns something you've been trying to say/do with your children's behaviour. This is linked back to how we ourselves were parented – if you and your partner had very different upbringings it may be that this will become very obvious when it comes to how you choose to discipline your own children, or even down to the types of routines that you feel comfortable with, the 'norms' that you assume in your family life: sit-down family Sunday lunch non-negotiable? Dinner in front of the TV a definite no-no?

It tends to happen that if one parent is very 'chilled out', the other may travel towards the other end of the spectrum. Without trying to find a middle ground, it can end up that one parent is very laid back and the other extremely strict, which can lead to feelings of 'ganging up' on one parent if the laid-back partner sides with their maligned little one.

Often it's dad who's too strict, but 'fun dad' syndrome may also arise, particularly if he doesn't spend much time with the kids – if he works a lot, or doesn't live in the family home, for example. In this scenario, dad doesn't want to taint the time he has with his children by telling them off, and wants to make all the time special and fun. Apart from anything else, this isn't real life, and there has to be a compromise found in order to create a balanced relationship – and prevent mum-resentment from festering.

Physical relationships

As we touched (if you'll excuse the pun) upon in the previous chapter, the physical side of a relationship can change dramatically. Exhaustion is to blame, combined with the physical and emotional fall-out of growing babies in your body, and the demands of life with children. Many women mutter darkly in the hours after giving birth that they are never, ever going anywhere near a penis ever again. Same-sex relationships suffer in exactly the same way: motherhood places heavy demands on body and mind. So it can take a while to put the va-va-voom back into the mix.

Follow all the suggestions given in Chapter 4 to find your mojo, and – as long as it feels right for you – actively encourage yourself to see in your partner the things that initially attracted you to them. Deliberately stoke those embers. It's important, it's fun, and it'll be worth it.

> 'Choose to love, every day. Thank your partner for tidying up. Come on to your other half even if you're tired and should really go to sleep. Send inappropriate texts the next day. Flirt. Hold hands. Hug often. Make yourself – even if you're fed up and tired. Physical closeness matters because it makes a difference. Just like with babies. It releases the oxytocin all relationships need to survive. Explain yourself – we are all different. Communicate. No one is a mind reader. Be clear, patient and kind.'
>
> Antonia, doula, antenatal teacher and mum of three

'It sounds silly but I didn't know how breastfeeding would change my relationship with my partner ... I breastfed both my kids until they were nearly two, and now I just can't see my boobs as being sexual any more, it feels wrong. And it's something that has really affected our relationship, he feels cheated because I just don't want him to touch them anymore.'

Steph, mum of two

Communication

In early 2017 a story was reported of a Japanese couple who didn't talk for 20 years. The husband uttered not a word to his partner, even while they were living together, bringing up three children. After all of this time – and it took their 18-year-old son writing to a reality TV show to uncover this – he revealed in his first words to her that he was giving her the cold shoulder out of jealously for the attention and care the children got from her. He was basically sulking. For 20 years.

Open and honest communication is vital in any relationship – and especially for parents. If there is constant tension:

- make time to talk when you're both feeling calm
- listen and (try to) understand your partner's perspective
- reframe your view of things to avoid constant criticism or blame.

Postnatal depression can affect both parents, and it has a huge impact on relationships. Supporting each other and finding help is really important.

Descending into silence can happen without you really noticing. Talk, like on those first dates where you talked all through the night about 'stuff'. Learn about each other again – you haven't stopped developing or experiencing life just because you're long-term partners, there may still be things to learn about each other.

Dealing with anger

We talked a bit about anger in Chapter 1. We all have shorter fuses when sleep, stress, children and dirty pants are in the mix. Finding healthy ways to deal with anger is essential to make sure you don't fall into unhelpful habits and patterns for your relationship.

'I feel terrible when I get unreasonably cross with them because I've had a bad day, and end up going in to their rooms at night and kissing them and telling them that I love them and vowing that I'll never do it again. Except I always do, because ultimately, I'm human and I'll keep making mistakes and that's OK, as long as you acknowledge those mistakes. Which is another life lesson I try and teach my kids!'

Hannah, mum of two

Scribble and stamp it out

This activity is for managing anger within your relationship.

In moments of teeth-gnashing anger, sometimes it's best to let the anger out rather than trying to calm it down. However, instead of allowing your rage to come out in venomous words or unhelpful thoughts, allow it to be channelled physically instead.

You can do this with your children as well as a way of letting them voice how they're feeling: it's a brilliant way of getting them to visually/physically depict their innermost feelings, which they may not otherwise be able to put into words.

Scribble:

- take your notepad and a pen/pencil
- scribble it out
- vent your frustration and rage on that piece of paper
- draw characters, or simply scribble incoherently to spread the anger into the paper and out of your head.

Stamp:

- stamp, jump and shout the anger out of your body
- you could shout and yell in a safe place by yourself
- drive out into the countryside, stand on the top of a hill, fill your lungs, and yell as loud as you can for as long as you can to release all that pent-up frustration.

Toddlers have the right idea – tantruming is a full-body experience because they have no real way of articulating their feelings in words. Sometimes this is more effective even when you do have words. So, allow yourself to jump up and down and stamp your feet.

When your parenting relationship hasn't worked

Of course, not everyone who is parenting is doing it within the two-biological-parents framework. You might be a step-parent, or a single mum. When a relationship has broken down it's important to recognise, if it was an unhealthy relationship, that it was *for the best* that it didn't continue. Your children will be infinitely better off within a healthy loving environment than within the crumbling structure of a live-in relationship that has broken down.

> 'When single parenthood was thrust upon me, though a difficult path it was to be, I lucked out with a pretty awesome family who respect me and have pretty similar opinions on how to raise a child. Motherhood to me means being happy, it means that when I go to bed exhausted, dragging my feet but happy that I am doing an OK job. It means not putting too much pressure on myself, being realistic.'
>
> Alex, mum of one

Supermum syndrome would have us believe that we are failing if we're not the most popular mum on the block, and that familial and friend relationships should be free from tension, be supportive, fun, nourishing and perfect, at all times. Sadly that isn't real life. Once we reconcile ourselves to the fact that relationships, like life, meander through phases, ebb and flow, ups and downs, we can more ably get on with the business of being a wonderful mum in our everyday life, without piling on the pressure to be all things to all people.

> 'If I've had a "good mothering day", it's down to me and the kids, not just me. So I congratulate all of us.'
>
> Hannah, mum of two

6

The school floodgates: navigating the mores from playground to PTA

This chapter brings you back to school. When our children start school it heralds a new era, saying an official goodbye to the baby days. They're now 'in the system', and your freedom to hang out with them whenever you like, and go away on holiday at the cheapest times of year, is fettered. It's a time of mixed emotions, bringing a whole load of new and complex social and psychological issues to face, for you and for your child. In this chapter we'll work through these various flashpoints, and offer you a toolkit of therapies to dip into to help you negotiate this time of flux and make sure that the school days are halcyon days.

Supermum arrives at the school gates on time, with bouncing, healthy, happy children bearing organic freshly made packed lunches. They're never in a rush or a grump, or a grumpy rush. She's on the PTA, the school run is her catwalk, she's the centre of a tight gaggle of mum friends. Her child is signed up for all the right after-school activities, and she never misses an assembly.

We sort of hate that supermum that we see looking so pristine and, well, sorted, while we're bleary eyed, with yesterday's knickers sticking out of the ankle of our jeans. But, rarely do we ponder the fact that we might have fictionalised her 'behind the scenes', judging our own in comparison to her final performance. We *don't* see her precariously put-together work–family jigsaw, her breakfast-while-getting-dressed-for-school-run – 'come-on, come-on!!' – morning assault course. The effort is going on below the water unseen as the swan glides serenely across the lake. She may appear poised and composed, but then, hey, you never know – so may you. You have no idea truly how you come across to others.

There's much editorial mileage to be gained from pitching mum 'types' against each other at the school gates: the smug supermum, the bitchy clique mum group, the PTA fierce mum. But, actually, perhaps we need to soften our gaze and realise that we're *all* muddling through – be it in pyjamas or in Chanel – and be a bit kinder to ourselves and each other.

Times of change

Possibly there was a sense of relief when your child began full-time education, not least because you're shelling out less money for childcare. Even so, when they hesitantly pottered through those school gates for the first time, tortoise-like with school bag on their back, it's unlikely that you didn't shed a tear. How is my baby suddenly so big? It seems like yesterday that I was grappling with banana purées ...

Mixed emotions of sadness/happiness come into play when your children go to school, and inexorably move up the one-way escalator of the academic system. Perhaps you feel a great sense of loss – your not-so-tiny baby is shedding their baby skin before your eyes.

And yet there's excitement and potential too – more time and freedom for you, plus the delight in seeing your little one hopefully thriving, excelling, learning and blossoming. Entering school is a monumental transition time, knocking that first domino of the education system that ultimately ends with our little fledglings leaving the nest, having sufficiently developed into proper humans ready to enter the world on their own.

Having children can be like watching a time-lapse video. Looking back, phases seem to have passed inordinately quickly, despite feeling like a hundred years when you were in the thick of them – colic, explosive nappies, tantrums, picking-your-battles, sleep, please, fricking sleep. How can this rainy day NOT BE OVER YET? In difficult demanding phases, mum life can feel like a heady cocktail of both wishing time away and mourning its loss once it's gone and you hadn't had the chance to say goodbye.

As we move through each stage of life – starting Reception, before you know it moving to 'big' school, maybe then trotting off to university, or forging their way into the adult scary working world – at each step we're relinquishing 'control' (hah!) and influence over our children gradually. We need to learn to frame this positively.

Quite simply, we need to pause, to recognise and welcome each step, rather than pressing that invisible fast-forward button in your head and seeing it all playing out before your eyes, anxious about it being gone – missing it while it's still here. If your child has just started Reception – yes, it does beckon in a new era, but try not to wish it away by being overly aware of all those other eras that come after. See what's right in front of you, not only what's waiting behind that.

Your changing mothering role

In these times of transition, the *tasks of parenting* also inevitably change. The needs of your baby were very different from those of your rampaging preschooler, and again from those of a school-age child ... a tween, teen, older adolescent. As parents, we are always taking into account our child's changing language, their cognitive, social and emotional abilities. Remember when you understood that a helium-voiced 'genku' meant 'thank you', and you didn't even notice when the words became properly articulated; the genku phase had passed.

As a mum, you're constantly, without even being aware, recalibrating your input and your relationship with your child. These transitions require complex levels of thought and action, and yet we don't stop to notice what an achievement it is that any of us can do it and still have the brain capacity to carry on with regular normality day to day (OK, with the occasional moment of putting your house keys in the freezer). It's like alchemy – every single day, complex things are happening – so it's no wonder these can be times when things often feel 'stuck' or incredibly stressful.

Sailing the sea of change

Anxiety is the biggest emotion that comes with change. Times of change bring uncertainty, which feels 'dangerous' and unchartered. As we've seen before, anxiety is a little alarm set to provoke us into action to escape from danger. We can expect to feel anxious at any of these transition points – so, reframe it by telling yourself that it's *completely natural*.

Professional athletes often reframe anxiety positively, to harness its power to help them get stronger. Olympic-medal-winner pentathlete, and mum, Jessica Ennis-Hill visualises the sensation of nervous butterflies in her stomach as a vast host of butterflies pulling her towards the finish line.

ACTIVITY

Visualise your emotion, harness it, release it

In your notebook, let your creative juices flow and have a go at drawing the challenging feelings that you are experiencing.

What picture/pictures come to you? They might be:

- human characters
- animals
- landscapes
- weather forces.

Manifesting your worries visually will help you to reframe your emotions into a more tangible, manageable entity. Looking at your picture, ask yourself what choices could you make to make this anxiety feel smaller and less scary.

Positive affirmations, self-talk

We can use positive self-talk to get us through this period of change (see page 125).

Say

You can voice your affirmations out loud to yourself, for example: 'I dealt with xxxx so I can deal with this', or, if your child is the one experiencing the most anxiety about transition, 'they dealt with nursery, so this is going to be OK.'

Write

Writing your self-talk affirmations on a card and sticking it somewhere obvious so that you can see it every day is a good way of ensuring that you feel the positive effects of these affirmations drip-feeding into your internal dialogue.

Draw

Perhaps draw your affirmations in lovely writing/a colourful pen and stick them on the fridge or in your bathroom, where you'll see them every morning.

Examples

Here are some self-talk affirmations you can use.

- 'I don't have to be perfect.'
- 'Today is a brand new day.'
- 'I am being the best mother I can be.'
- 'I let go of things that I can't control.'
- 'Every mistake is an opportunity to grow and learn.'
- 'I am everything my child needs.'

Marathon, not a sprint

In these moments of turbulence, where the rhythm of your life is disturbed and you're trying to get used to the new groove, it's worth occasionally reminding ourselves of 'the long game' – the aim of parenting is not just that moment's task, to be able to grapple with your eight-year-old's maths homework without losing the plot, it's ultimately to produce a fully functioning, balanced adult who can slot into society happily.

These periods of transition turn up the dial of a dimmer switch, appropriately encouraging each step on your child's road to independence. Viewing periods of change like this – seeing them as essential challenges to help develop the survival skills our children need for adult life – will make them easier to negotiate.

Happy days?

The school era can bring back your own school experiences. Great news if you loved school and it was one of life's high points ... but if it was a less than wonderful experience for you, this might be more of a challenge. There's nothing like walking into a classroom to cast you back to the whole sensory experience of what that was like for you. If your own school experience was difficult, this may make it harder for you when your child starts school. If that's the case, try to stay in the moment while you are there.

ACTIVITY

Sensory schooling

If we found school anxiety-provoking as a child, we can get caught up in perpetuating this as an adult – allowing it to grow rather than diminish. This is an exercise that can help you work through old childhood memories, and bring together the adult and child you.

Focus on a particular part of a classroom or playground, and then focus on the *here and now*, to reinforce your understanding that you are *not* back at school. The following techniques guide you through doing this mentally and physically.

- Mentally repeat to yourself specific details of the current situation, e.g. 'the wall is yellow, the carpet is blue'.

- Put a hand on a wall, or sit on a chair, to help stabilise yourself – especially if you are very anxious in a school environment. The feel of something solid is a good reminder that you are in the present moment.

- Tell yourself repeatedly, 'I am in the present, I am bigger/more confident/in control now'.

Your child self 'meeting' your adult self

Find two photos: a school photo and one of you as an adult.

- Take the time to notice the differences between you.
- Remind yourself that you have a whole host of new skills, resources, talents and abilities.
- Write down these skills and talents.
- Take a minute to think about what would have helped the 'child you' at that time – what sort of support or encouragement would have made a difference?
- Tell her how you would have helped, had you been there as an adult.

Transactional Analysis – the 'child' ego state

Your child going to school is one of the things that can make you feel more intensely 'adult' than at any other time in your mothering journey thus far. Suddenly there's a huge sense of responsibility to make sure that you stick up for things that you feel very strongly about: the school's ethos, your child's rights, making sure things are running smoothly, fairly and well.

If you're not used to fighting even your own corner, you can feel quite helpless as to how to deal with this additional pressure of fighting your child's adequately.

Ever wonder why you sometimes feel like you've reverted back to being a small child in certain situations ... or maybe a sulky teenager when you're at your parents' house, even if you're 41 years old? The psychologist Eric Berne developed the concept of Transactional Analysis in the late 1950s. He identified three *ego-states* that exist during what he termed every 'transaction' between people – a transaction being, simply, a conversation, or an exchange of words or gestures.

These three 'ego-states' described different parts of our personalities, each one reflecting the thoughts, feelings and behaviours that determine how we express ourselves, interact with others and form relationships. They are outlined below.

- **Parent** – thoughts, feelings and behaviours learnt from our parents and other important people in our lives. This part of our personality can be *supportive or critical.*
- **Adult** – direct responses in the *'here and now'*, i.e. not influenced by our past. This tends to be the most rational part of our personality.
- **Child** – thoughts, feelings and behaviours *learnt from our childhood.* These can be inherently yours, or strongly adapted to parental influences.

All people subtly interchange their ego-states during the course of all 'transactions'. These changes aren't necessarily even verbal – they can be facial expressions or body language. So, for example, you could be talking with your partner about the shopping, and something they say triggers you to respond in your child ego-state. You may then both subtly enter different roles – they might take on the 'parent' to your 'child' in that transaction, if you feel criticised perhaps. And you might respond as 'child', either verbally or, simply, in your body language.

It is interesting to try to notice these roles in your key relationships. If you notice yourself 'telling off' your partner, or responding in a sulky – even tantrumy – way to them, it might be worth looking at what has brought this role out in you. Ideally, both partners in a conversation would take adult roles, as this is the most productive state to be in. It is really helpful (and, admittedly, tough) to learn the art of noticing a switch and then bring yourself back to an adult role.

As with any change, this may not be an easy process. Your core beliefs will always want to reroute you back on track to your habitual responses if you're finding it hard work. But think about the butterfly that emerges from its cocoon. There's a lot of pushing and grunting that goes on to make that cocoon break up. Be prepared to do the work, and new positive emotional habits can emerge. Can you imagine if the caterpillar felt too shy or scared to push its way out? There would be no butterfly. Don't deny the world your butterfly.

Who's the adult here ...?

You may find yourself unsure of how to communicate effectively with the headteacher – for example, if there are things you're not clear or happy about with the school's policies, or how they have dealt with your child. Experiences in the head's office in our own childhoods can mean we easily slip into the 'child' ego-state with your child's headteacher. We need to focus on keeping these conversations as 'adult'–'adult'.

I once had to approach the head at my son's school about the state of the loos – they were worse than any festival toilet I'd been in (and that's saying quite a lot) – and a few of the kids were reluctant to go as a result, with obvious consequences. Although, rationally, I knew that I was legitimately unhappy about it, I felt myself blushing red and quaking in my boots a bit while talking to him, and definitely didn't place myself on equal adult footing to him.

Knowing that subconsciously this could happen, try writing some notes to help you remember what you really want to say. It's even a good idea to think through your best outcome before the meeting so that you have more of a picture of what you want from it.

Think about your posture – 'Wonder Woman' stance (see page 107) is useful here – and allow your posture to feed into your confidence that you *are* an adult, and have legitimate concerns that should be listened to.

Ask your mentor

This is a helpful activity to do if you find yourself having to face a difficult situation.

- Spend some time visualising people in your life who have been great mentors, coaches and encouragers.
- Bring one to mind.
- In your difficult situation, imagine, 'What would xxxx say?' and, most importantly, 'How would xxxx say it?'
- The key is to get the tone right, be able to emulate and channel some of your mentor's wisdom, confidence and style – gentle and nurturing when needed, and also galvanising and encouraging.

ACTIVITY

Social butterfly, or solo bee?

School days inherently reawaken your own experiences of making friends. It might be that primary school was your zenith – you were queen of the playground, and you made friends that you still meet with for coffees and luxury mini breaks (OK, walks around the local park). Or perhaps, for you, it was all about secondary school. Maybe your whole school journey was tinted by social anxiety in some way? It's important not to place your social anxieties onto your child – and also try to understand if your child is a different social 'type' to you.

Beware of passing your own anxieties about popularity on to your child by worrying about their social 'ranking' – are they cool/popular, are they an introvert? Notice if you're constantly apologising for them in social situations and labelling them shy, when actually they might simply be cautious and discerning. Children will pick up pretty much everything you emanate around your concerns about them.

Are you projecting your own supermum popularity expectations onto your child? If they don't seem to be invited on play dates, or, perhaps worse still, not invited to the 'right' play dates, check in with yourself to see whether you have *their* interests truly at the heart of your worries, or whether you're tapping into your own core-belief system of being unpopular or unworthy.

If your child is content – and make sure you regularly connect with them to elicit this rather than presume or pre-empt – then try to acquiesce and respond to their social forays at school rather than push what you feel is better for them. It's not easy, but aim to move past your own framework; try not to put pressure on your child, but go with their own friendship choices.

> '*I'm embarking on this next step of the parenting journey like a 14-year-old girl – I just want to fit in, I want the school mums to like me, to like my child, to invite him on play dates.*'
>
> Emma, mum of two

> '*The "perfect mums" at school make me feel crap. The ones who know each other, know the teachers and who walk home*

*with the kids together. The ones with lots of questions at
parents' forums and whose children are overachieving. I always
think I'm failing in some way as I'm not doing that and part of
the "gang".'*

Debbie, mum of two

*'I went through a phase of being very conscious that my son
wasn't being invited on any play dates. I'd notice that other
mums would wander off after school together having arranged
to play, and Oscar was never included. He is on the autistic
spectrum and I know he's quite a "difficult", challenging
character in their class, but it made me so sad that no one was
prepared to make the effort and see beyond his condition to
get to know him.'*

Kate, mum of three

Any cliques and judgements we thought we'd left behind at school can
pop up again for us with our children. We might suddenly feel hyper
aware that we're not in the 'cool' mums crew, within the 'A list'. Try to
revisit what we've learnt about our automatic thoughts and core
beliefs (see page 43) and realise that you are *creating* this truth, and it
might actually not be the case.

Everyone is pushed for time and feeling a bit frazzled on the school run;
the chances of you being deliberately ostracised are slim. Focus on the
present moment – your child's school experience rather than your own
– and all that we discussed about friendships in the previous chapter,
and things will gradually slot into place.

Good enough?

Do you have certain phrases from your own school reports etched in
your memory? Either because they gave you a warm glow, or because
they made you sting in a way that has stayed with you ever since (and
possibly reinforced negative core beliefs)? These feelings can be echoed
when your child is thrust into this new realm of being regularly
evaluated and judged. It can be really hard not to let anxious feelings
take hold about your child not performing as well as others in his class,
or as well as he 'should' be for his age.

The terminology used in your child's reports seeps inevitably into your own understanding and judgement of your child's abilities – almost placing a barrier between you and observing your child at face value. Our children from the tiddly age of four (and even earlier) are graded on the criteria of 'emerging/expected/exceeding'.

This taps into often deep-seated insecurities about not being good enough compared to the next person, creating a real fear of lagging behind. Or, whether you like it or not, there might be a sharp pang of 'hmm, why isn't my daughter EXCEEDING? Why is she just plain NORMAL? This can't be right – she's EXCEPTIONAL!' The language of competition is so key here, and hard to ignore, along with the accompanying feeling of winning or losing.

More than words

The school-based language revolves around 'what is expected', which seems to feed into a general social narrative of 'not good enough' for parents and children. This is developed even more in the language around schools' 'performance' and in league tables. But *who* has created this benchmark that we're judged against?

Do you even know whose expectations our children are striving/failing to meet? Do you understand and respect entirely the criteria that are used? Are we trying to fit lots of different shapes into one hole? We're not entirely clear about that side of it, yet we still allow ourselves to feel judged by it, and inadequate. If we don't even know who we're trying to impress, how can it be a shared expectation?

It's important to have an understanding of the criteria framework before you allow yourself to feel berated or deflated by the vocabulary used. If you entirely respect and wholeheartedly uphold the judgements that are placed on your individual child, then yes, it has some value for you.

I personally had a wobble when my firstborn kept coming up 'small' on the Red Book chart of fear when he was a baby. He was always well under the fiftieth centile – making me feel bad that he was so teeny tiny, it was 'my fault'. It made me feel anxious, and that I was underachieving, worried about his health and robustness and ability to thrive. I only began to shed this feeling when I learnt that these centiles are created by the World Health Organisation to 'show the position of a measured parameter within a statistical distribution. *They do not show if that parameter is normal or abnormal. They merely show how it compares with that measurement in other individuals'.*

Understanding that the measurement wasn't showing a 'right versus wrong', despite the congratulatory tone of pride you hear when people talk of being awarded a place on the one-hundredth centile, I realised that perhaps I shouldn't take it as a judgement of my mothering abilities.

In a similar vein – school league tables and reports are an arbitrary framework applied to all children, not taking into account any learning nuances, special quirks, delightful talents and unique joys that you as mum are privy to in your child. So, you shouldn't allow the vocabulary of general statistics to colour/dampen your belief in and optimism about your child's achievements, or your achievements as a mother.

The competitive parenting trap

The general atmosphere of league tables and reports only adds fuel to the easily stoked embers of competitive parenting – leaving you with a constant nagging feeling that you're just not good enough.

Competitive parenting is there, lurking behind the home-made sugar-free madeleines that yogic mum made for the school fundraising coffee morning, or in a smiling #humblebrag about reading levels or test prowess. Whatever its guise, competitive parenting usually leads you to doubt yourself, your child, your approach.

In the framework of a chaotic, sleep-deprived (i.e. 'normal parenting') day, seemingly innocent comments can hit you like a ton of bricks:

'He's been walking since he was six months. He spoke early too. So I wasn't surprised when the teacher told me his writing was well ahead of the rest of the class.' OR

'It was really *embarrassing* – the headteacher said that Alfie's French is better than hers, and she lived in France for ten years!' OR

'What's *PAW Patrol*? We don't own a TV.'

Press pause: mindful awareness

You're most likely to feel affected by an anxious competitive thought or school-gate supermum comment when you're feeling under par and less in touch with your automatic thoughts.

Take a moment to pause: breathe and check in with your body. Are you particularly exhausted, stressed, or having 'one of those days' where the rhythm isn't right? If so, take a deep breath, stand up tall, and imagine literally shrugging off unhelpful comments and thoughts, as a little bird would shrug off raindrops.

As we touched on in the last chapter (see page 134), if you feel stung by competitive comments from another mum, remember that they will ultimately have stemmed from her seeking reassurance of her way of doing things. And if you feel a competitive thought rising up in yourself, swallow it and try to explore *why* you're feeling competitive – whom exactly does it serve? Why do you feel the need to ask your friend what level of reading her four-year-old is on? Is it so that you get to feel smug knowing that your child is doing better? Or is it so that you can feel anxious that your child is falling behind? Are you simply hoping to reassure yourself that you're both in the same boat?

Crouching tiger, hidden supermum

Notice if your naturally competitive nature is manifesting in an urge to compete through your children. Parents are under unprecedented pressure now to try to ensure our children 'keep up' with their peers, and collectively ensure that their school is at the top of the league tables. As a result of mounting cultural pressure to be a 'tiger parent', do some of us push our children too far or expect too much?

Increased tutoring, back-to-back after-school activities, play dates and endless testing means there's less space than ever for children to be free, to find flow in play – even simply to be bored so that creativity can exist in that unfilled space. Psychologists, teachers and health professionals are reporting increases in childhood depression and anxiety, partly as a direct response to this pressure.

Try to silence the ticker tape loop of competitive comments and thoughts (your own and others'). Breathe through the temptation to compare to others when it's your child on the pedestal. We need to focus on building our child's confidence irrespective of others' achievements, foster their healthy work ethic – and surely give them tools for a joyful life above all.

Keep your faith in yourself as a parent even when it's knocked by a careless comment, and always maintain a sense of perspective. Send your children a really important message: that you care about them as individuals, and your affection is not linked to their achievements.

This message to your kids becomes ever more important as the school system becomes increasingly competitive. Within an atmosphere of mounting pressure and competition, as mums we have to at least try to ensure that home provides solace and a feeling of unconditional support: a constant oxygen boost to a deflated balloon – even if it means suppressing our own supermum ambitions for vicarious greatness.

'There is always competition where women are.'

Cee, mum of two

Who's that supermum?

There's undoubtedly a mum at the school gates who makes it look effortless, who makes your kids look like a rowdy rabble, who makes you inwardly cringe at your appearance/tardiness/life. But, what do you really know about her?

> *'I'm a realist and I honestly think we all struggle, despite what some mothers try and make us believe. I often think the ones who look like they're coping brilliantly might well be the ones who need the most help.'*

Hannah, mum of two

If you look like you are the supermum coping brilliantly, it's likely that no one will offer to help – and why would they, when you've got it covered with such aplomb? On the contrary, as you're such a whizz they'll probably be asking you to do it for them too – are you the mum who somehow has committed to picking up ten kids from school for a play date on your own because you are just so brilliant at entertaining the kids? Or the one who is always organising the class end-of-term presents for the teachers because it's just expected of you now, since you did it so wonderfully the first time that no one else could compete?

Without any offers of help, you'll have to carry on doing it brilliantly alone – to the bar that you raised so high all by yourself. Often, trying to do everything on your own is underpinned by thoughts like, 'asking for help is weak/needy', perhaps combined with a family history of belief that 'coping with everything independently is a sign of strength.'

This can lead to the supermum in question learning over time that 'others are not helpful' or 'others do not care', or, simply, 'my needs are not as important as those of others.' This therefore leads to her being a martyr to her cause and carrying on by herself, trying to do everything independently. The underlying beliefs are then constantly being perpetuated, in an ongoing cycle.

Does this ring true for you? If you recognise in yourself that you find it hard to let that guard down, to be vulnerable and show the world any signs of imperfection or ask for a hand, perhaps it's time to raise the curtain on your 'behind the scenes'. That way, you're likely to open important communication and make connections that will lessen the burden on you, and ultimately make life easier *and more enjoyable* ... even if it means that people might discover your secret jumbo stash of chocolate fingers that you use to help coerce your children into compliance occasionally.

Am I enough?

Do you find yourself worrying constantly about something you're not doing that is contributing towards your child 'failing' at school/in life – not putting in enough time after school on practising writing; not signing up for enough after-school clubs; not doing *more* than the rest of the class? Worrying without action is like always holding an umbrella, even on sunny days, just waiting for it to rain.

It may seem counterintuitive, but people who excel at worrying are not so good at putting this into useful action to overcome their worry. The worry creates stress, which closes down creativity and your perceived ability to cope with the problem. Action involves *working out the possible steps to overcome the problem*, then working on each step in turn – even if it means baby steps. So, if you're genuinely worried, *do* something about it. Read more with your child. Sign them up for the clubs if you can. Or just don't worry about it.

Do you worry about your child not having enough 'stuff' compared to their classmates? Nowhere is this more visible than at class birthday parties, which seem increasingly to be a competition for achieving supermum status: what used to be pretty much no-frills gatherings of chocolate-hungry children have now morphed into expectations of Oscar-worthy spectacles and themed events/experiences, with hundreds spent on party bags, costumes, the cake, etc. The pressure stems from what is expected, without a look at what is actually necessary, and, arguably, most fun.

Focus on your fears

ACTIVITY

Let's experiment by testing out some of the things that cause you anxiety about what you might not be doing enough of/have too high expectations about for yourself/your child.

In your notebook, note down the two main things that cause you stress and anxiety in terms of your child's school experience – things that you are worried about. Then, try to play out your scenario to test out what exactly would happen if you allowed the boundaries to be tested. Here are two examples.

1) Your anxiety is your child's performance at school, which translates as them not ever missing a day.

- Think about your fears. Why is it so important to you that they never miss a day, even if they might be feeling under the weather?

- Try to pay attention to all the information around, not just that which supports the belief you have.

- Once you can identify your fears and know where they have come from, you could test them out and actually rock your own internal boat a little. For example, the next time your child is ill, let them stay off for one day more than you normally would.

- Notice what happens. Take this as a test of whether your child can miss one day of school and *not fail, not get into trouble*; notice whether it's also the case that *you don't get into trouble*.

2) Your anxiety is parties.

- What are your anxieties about your child's parties? Deliberately test out some of them. Make a conscious choice to have a small budget, not spend more than a couple of hours planning, only have three other children, get a cake from Tesco, even do away with party bags.

- Thinking about doing any of these things may provoke a response from you, so, first, pay attention to this.

- Ask yourself why any of these things are important to you?

- It could be because your anxiety is that your child will be unpopular without them, or because they (or most likely you) will be judged to be 'tight' or 'not good enough'.

- These thoughts may well relate to your memories of childhood, as well as your experiences or fears about the parents and friends of your child now. Weigh up the situation by taking into account all of the information around.

- You may identify a fear as, 'I am worried that my child (I) will not be liked if they don't have an expensive party.' Think about how you will know afterwards if they are not liked (what evidence there will be – perhaps it's that they won't be invited to anyone else's party, or you won't be invited anywhere). Then be brave, and test it out.

Remember that any competition is really about you, the adult: children will be happy as long as there is cake, games/dancing/general chaos, and some element of 'going-home present' (when I was little it was all about the going-home present, which was usually a bag with a sticker in it – it's all about the novelty rather than the actual gift) or party bag.

Spending thousands on a Pinterest-worthy theme will probably be lost on the kids but will be throwing a gauntlet down to any potential parental competition that might be simmering. If you truly love to prepare and thrive on throwing a huge bash, absolutely go for it. But if you're motivated by showing off to the other adults, maybe take a good honest look at your reasons why.

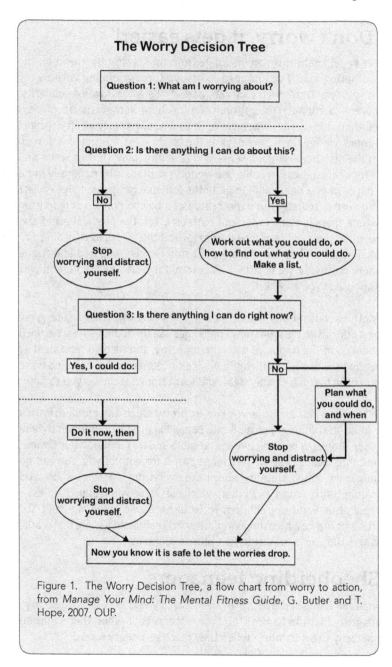

Figure 1. The Worry Decision Tree, a flow chart from worry to action, from *Manage Your Mind: The Mental Fitness Guide*, G. Butler and T. Hope, 2007, OUP.

'Don't worry, it gets easier!'

We've all heard this rosy message from mums slightly ahead on the mothering road. I've said it to so many mums grappling with messy early days: 'Don't worry, it gets easier!' It's a message of solidarity, hope – a friendly recognition of how hard some aspects of new motherhood can be. When we're in that heady snotty sleep-deprived tunnel, we see the school days as the bright light shining as a beacon in the distance – when a sense of 'normality' may start to settle and things become less frenetic. Less frenetic, perhaps. And definitely more chance of you being able to go to the loo unaccompanied. But easier? We need to manage our expectations of a halcyon future of parenting where there is calm, order and harmony. Yes, the physical grind and relentlessness of the early days passes. But this is replaced by different challenges. Unless we can alter our mindset, be prepared and frame them positively, we're left with a resounding sense of 'I thought it was supposed to be EASIER?!'

Motherhood morphs through each phase: certain things fade away and difficulties pass, but new challenges rise up in their stead. We need to let go of the notion of it becoming *easier*, and instead reframe it as rising to each fresh challenge a bit like surfing: each challenge is a wave you have to catch exactly right, and learn from if it causes you to flop.

When your kids are little, you can fix pretty much any problem with a cuddle (and, failing that, a biscuit/Peppa Pig plaster). But when they're older, problems become more intangible and less immediately fixable, and this means that the parameters shift for both of you. You can no longer be 'magic mummy' and make everything OK with a kiss and cuddle. It takes more than that, which can leave you feeling helpless – none of us want our children to be unhappy, so when we can't 'fix' things it can be a heartbreaking time of transition to a more real world, where they have to start to face proper 'problems'.

Shepherding teenagers

A paper published in 2016 in the journal *Developmental Psychology* suggests that the hardest time for mothers isn't when their children are teeny tiny, but later – when they reach secondary school.

The paper, conducted by Arizona State University, reports the findings from a survey of American mothers. The participants responded to a series of questions designed to assess multiple facets of their wellbeing, including stress and life satisfaction, perceptions of their child's behaviour and aspects of their experiences as a parent, such as feelings of guilt and being subsumed by parenthood.

In the early years, when motherhood is undoubtedly acutely physically demanding, mothers reported high levels of parenting 'overload' – we all know that time, when you always have a small person touching you in some way, and usually leave the house with porridge in your hair. Mums during this period felt that mothering crowded out time and energy for themselves, and, as we've seen in Chapter 5, eclipsed other elements of their identities, swamped their sense of self.

But, happily, they also reported high levels of positive behaviours from their children – after all, this is the time of the most cuteness you can possibly absorb (think chunky cheeks, squeaky voices, giggles that make your insides throb with loving feelings) and generally high levels of 'parenting satisfaction' overall. This suggests that the early challenges of motherhood are high but are offset by correspondingly high rewards: there's a lot of take but also a hell of a lot of give.

By the time those edible toddlers reached adulthood, the surveyed mothers reported much lower levels of 'parenting overload' and guilt, but happily also maintained relatively high levels of parenting satisfaction. Contrary to the idea that mothers suffer from 'empty nest' syndrome, the data from this survey suggested that mums of adult children enjoy quite high levels of maternal wellbeing: there's perhaps less palpable worry and logistical chaos around your kids day to day, and more time for work, yoga, book clubs, anything that makes you feel like 'you' again.

Between these two periods, in the early adolescent period, mothers reported the highest levels of dissatisfaction with parenting, with mothers of younger secondary-school children representing the peak. Interestingly, it's not just about the parenting – life satisfaction also dipped in this period, with highs in stress, loneliness and 'feelings of emptiness'. Mothers with school children also tended to perceive more negative behaviours from their children – this is the age when emotional turbulence isn't accompanied by wonderful cuddle-thons, but instead with a movement away from parental attachment.

'I always feel like I want to defend teenagers from how society views them. My daughters are a challenge, and it's very hard to get the right mix of boundary, guidance, trust and acceptance. But when you do it's wonderful. The transition for parent and child into the teenage years feels like a rocky road, and is incredibly difficult to get right. But it can be rewarding and joyous. As a family we're in it together. We need to celebrate this amazing time in our children's lives, not constantly fear and criticise it.'

Julie, mum of two

'Teenagers are fun! They are the Beat poets, the Van Goghs, the avant-garde. They feel everything deeply and passionately. They're just trying to figure it all out, and we need to try and figure it out with them, and remember what it was like before we became the bumbling idiot parents.'

Maria, mum of two

'It sometimes feels like a military manoeuvre, thinking ahead of my daughter and deciding what really matters, picking the right battles. Attempting to be balanced and measured at all times. Bolstering her self-confidence. Providing safety. Being the grown-up.'

Louise, mum of one

This age is a challenging time to be a mum, to negotiate this heady territory of puberty, with its dipping toes into risky behaviour, pushing boundaries to grapple with developing new identity. This particularly tricky time for mums reflects the fact that it is also a tricky time for children. This is the age when children are most likely to be referred for psychological help, with increases in anxiety and low mood notable in this age group.

It may highlight the whole family being under stress most at this time of life. For children, this age is when they become much more aware of the world around them, but also realise the limitations of their abilities:

the whole graded and tested nature of school life, which we've already touched on, coming into play in terms of influencing self-esteem and feelings of self-worth and achievement – which particularly increases the chance of them becoming anxious.

Mindfulness for teens

Being a teen can be really stressful. Mindfulness is a powerful way to handle stress – it's about living fully in the present moment, with an attitude of kindness. Breathing, noticing what's happening right here and now, sending a gentle Buddha-esque smile to whatever you're experiencing in this moment (whether it's easy or difficult), and then letting it go.

Practising mindfulness with your teenagers – or setting up a habit of practising with your young children and pre-teens – is a brilliant tool for allowing them to negotiate this new terrain, but also, crucially, can allow you a bit of space to connect and keep your lines of communication open with each other.

Teaching adolescents mindfulness techniques is sort of like giving them the instruction booklet for their own brains. Teenagers love learning about the workings of things. Teach them that mindfulness can help the rational, thinking part of the brain process raw emotion, which can ultimately lead to better decision making. It gives them a tool where they are able to notice when they need to pause and reflect – leading to a skillful response instead of a kneejerk unthinking, emotional, reaction.

Meditation has been shown to increase grey matter in the portion of the brain responsible for self-awareness and compassion. It can actually play a role in the neuroplasticity of the brain – blow your child's mind by telling them that our *experiences actually transform our brains, the way exercise transforms our bodies.*

Monkey mind

As we've seen when we looked at our automatic thoughts, we sometimes have little active awareness of the direction our thoughts take. With your

---

child/teen, it can be helpful to use the analogy of the monkey mind to help them understand their thought processes: monkeys constantly jumping around from branch to branch, thought to thought.

We can learn, with our children, how to press pause on the monkey mind's swinging – to be still before jumping to the next branch. This is often eye-opening – look at the journey you've been on within this book. Wouldn't it be amazing if we could give our kids the tools to avoid getting stuck on the wrong thought tree, but to pause and climb down for a moment?

Try these activities together, every day, or even just once a week. Commit regularly to it and you will both feel the benefits.

ACTIVITY

Mindfulness with your child/ teenager

Explain to your child that they can use these daily mindfulness strategies when they're feeling anxious, moody, angry, or just need to relax. They're perfect to give them ways to manage everyday stressors: school demands, worry, sadness, problems with relationships, difficulties focusing.

Gratitude journal

Encourage your child to spend two to three minutes a day thinking about one or two things to be grateful for. You can do this activity along with your child, so you will benefit too!

- Make sure that the list is different every day, and keep it simple.
- This helps foster gratitude for the simplest, everyday things that we often take for granted.
- This is powerful and effective because you are helping your child to train their brain to see the world differently, to look for the positive.
- It's important to be specific: if your child is grateful for their best friend, encourage them to write more than 'I feel grateful for my best friend.' Have them think about something their best friend does for which they're particularly grateful, e.g. 'I'm grateful that my best friend makes me laugh.'

- Being more specific helps the brain to create new patterns of optimism and positivity.

Happiness jar

This routine will help your child realise that they feel happiness along with their other emotions – it's just that they might not notice this as easily.

- Put a glass jar, along with blank slips of paper, in a place in your home where family members spend most of their time.
- When something good happens, however big or small, encourage your child to write it down, along with the date, and how this made your child feel.
- When the jar is full/at the end of the month/year/etc., open the jar and read the slips together.

Breathing exercises

Breathing – so important, so simple, and can be done anywhere. It is a really valuable tool to offer your child to get them through life's stormy moments.

- Sit with your child on the sofa, or propped up in a bed.
- Encourage your child to place their hands, folded, on their stomach.
- Ask them to take a deep breath in, and to watch their stomach and hands rise and fall with each breath.
- Encourage your child to imagine filling a balloon in their stomach with the air.
- Focus both of your minds on the breath, and let any thoughts drift away.
- If your child is struggling with thoughts, it may be helpful to focus on repeating a word with each breath, such as 'relax', 'calm', or 'peace'.

Breathing exercises are helpful to increase mindfulness and relaxation, and help children (and us) cope with troubling emotions, such as anxiety, anger and depression. Encourage your child to practise breathing exercises when feeling calm, and they will be more likely to be able to breathe when feeling frustrated or angry.

Safe from harm

One of the things that we hold most sacred in our parenting manifesto is keeping our children safe. To a certain extent, when they're little this is the easiest job because we have the most physical control over where they go and how they get there. But once they start to disentangle themselves from our grasp, that's when it can get slippery. That can cause huge amounts of worry and anxiety in this new phase of parenting – trying to get the balance right between never wanting to let them out of your sight, and wanting to be the 'cool' mum who all your child's friends envy.

The social landscape that teens are growing up in now is so different from the one that we grew up in that this can leave us wondering how on earth we set about protecting our child from situations that we have no experience in ourselves. This can lead to huge feelings of anxiety about protecting your teenager from online bullying, etc.

If your child is in secondary school, they might automatically and naturally get a bit defensive when you try to talk to them about internet safety: you're the boring mum and you're crossing boundaries, and generally being an overbearing parent. That's to be expected (cue eye roll). But, you do need to stubbornly keep this line of communication open with as much good nature as you can, as a safety line for your child.

Discussing internet safety in a calm and cool manner is likely to, however they react in the moment, ensure that your teenager feels comfortable about the issue, and opens their eyes to possible dangers. Maintain an open dialogue, always encourage your child to talk to you about their internet use, who they're talking to, what apps they're using. This definitely increases the chances of them approaching you if and when they run into trouble online.

Teens today face all sorts of new frontiers for worry compared to our school days: one out of three children will experience cyberbullying. A quarter of teens claim sexting is frequent, and 'normal'. Over half of teenagers feel that it is safe to post photos or intimate details online.

All a bit overwhelming, right? Rather than nestle into anxious thoughts about this, instead create a few strategies to find a balance and sense of safety within your home. The following are good habits to get into, for all the family:

- Create technology havens where the screens have to be turned off – bedrooms, bathrooms, or the family dinner table. This offers your teen a chance to unplug.
- Power down at set times. The whole family places their phones in a basket by the front door, not to be picked up until the morning.
- Create house rules or a contract with your teen about phone and internet use. Include the entire family equally, and negotiate the terms in a family meeting to make sure everyone is satisfied.

Remember that your teen is still a child, still learning, still developing their resilience and responses to experiences – although probably don't say that to their face if you don't want to irk them. As Robert Munsch's classic book *Love You Forever* goes, 'As long as I'm living/my baby you'll be.' Maintain sight of that love, that *like*, every day if you can.

Everyone makes mistakes – we've all made a shedload and I'm sure would prefer not to be judged for them. Part of growing up is learning from those experiences. Just as we're learning not to place supermum expectations on ourselves, we have to offer our kids the same courtesy and not place unreal demands on them.

Connecting with your child

You have a chance to see your child in a completely different light if you ask them to teach you about something they have learnt at school. By putting them in an expert position, you're helping them to experience a different side of themselves and of your relationship.

Children are rarely placed in a position of superior knowledge, so to allow them this can be very powerful. It's even better if it really is something you know absolutely nothing about so they get to call you ignorant, justifiably, and enlighten you.

If you're trying to connect with your children and a conversation about school isn't going down too well, then try something they might be more interested in. Try to offer them leads they can grab, to walk you through into their world, on their terms. These could be: technology, who they like to watch on YouTube, what games they play with friends, what books they love. Don't be too eager with your questions, otherwise we'll wander into overbearing territory (eye roll) – instead, truly listen, let go of control, and let them take the lead in what they want to say.

The school era is an age of huge transition, development, loss and gains. By making your focus all about your child and how they are interacting with the world, and viewing the school experience through their lens, you can begin to soften your supermum judgements and expectations of yourself, and free up more time for your relationship to grow and flourish.

7

Supermum meets super career: work that works?

This chapter will take you to the water cooler, to chat about the conundrum that is balancing work, life, family, sanity. Finding that balance as a working mum – or in choosing *not* to work/acquiescing to the fact that finding suitable work seems unfeasible while your kids are growing up – is a deeply personal, and hugely emotive, issue. Sometimes it can seem that there are just too many avenues to failure. And that's when self-doubt, anxiety and self-criticism can come to the fore, stubbing the toe of even the most heroic of supermums.

We will introduce some therapies that will allow you to unpack the things that might *not* be working very well, in order to review and try to construct your vision of a working life that offers peace, balance and stability (not to mention enough money to keep you and your children in new shoes) while maintaining your mental health.

Ultimately, we're searching for the reassurance that we're not abandoning our children if we need, or want, to work: that we're doing our best for them, and ourselves – that we're doing a good-enough job. We need to soften our opinion on 'perfection' and look instead to find that elusive balance – be fully true to yourself and what you believe is the right thing for you to do, as a mum, and as *you* – in whatever way we can.

The working mother is modern life's ultimate plate spinner. Each morning she rushes to various childcare drop-offs while simultaneously applying lipstick and making dentist appointments. She kisses her kids goodbye, swallowing the anguish of her toddler but wearing it like a heavy coat all day. She's constantly aware of an all-pervasive pressure to be the perfect parent in the tiny window she has before the working day. Rush, rush, rush. Help! Is this all there is to life?

> 'The obligation for working mothers is a very precise one: the feeling that one ought to work as if one did not have children, while raising one's children as if one did not have a job.'
>
> Annabel Crabb, political journalist

Career is the arena in which we are most in danger of falling into a supermum pothole. 'Super career women' often become affected by the quest to be a 'perfect' mum – it's just like a career shift applying the same skillset, ambitions and energy in a different way – albeit with more glitter and more volatile colleagues. So when the time comes where we need to combine both of our 'careers', this can lead to a real car crash for our wellbeing. A constant wrestle between two heavyweights: guilt and ambition. We're expected to excel equally at working and motherhood, but this is like spreading too little butter on too much toast.

The pressure for us to succeed on all fronts is making us wring ourselves out in an effort not to let any side down. This superhero striving for perfection at home and work means the bar is set unrealistically high. In this environment the two big arch-enemies to good-enough motherhood, guilt and anxiety, have free rein to run amok in our vulnerable minds.

Modern life is not cheap. Unless we want to live in a shack in the woods, eating bugs and leaves, someone in the household *needs* to work to have enough money to pay for things to eat, wear and, importantly, make our lives merry. But we might also love our job, and really *want* to do it, and then feel fettered and thwarted by the demands of our children. Children affect our pursuit of career goals in the sheer logistics and never-ending obligations they present, and they also deeply affect our desire for more of a work–life balance and flexibility in our working lives.

Lucy Jones, in her 2017 article *Longed-For Child*, said of the work/ mothering conundrum: 'Will I ever feel un-split again? I love my child, but I love my work, too. I'm vexed by the tension. I am surprised by the subliminal, contradictory messages I seem to have internalised, that a) modern motherhood is low-status drudgery that plucks a woman out of the "real world" and consigns her, voiceless, to the sidelines and b) mothers are selfish to go back to work (the "real world") because it will harm the child (whether they can afford not to remains beside the point). I reject these facile, rubbish notions, but still wonder where they came from.'

> 'One of the things I find hardest is that there isn't any help for us not to feel like we're being both a ropey mum and a ropey colleague. I feel like we need to talk about it more, as a society.'
>
> Louise, mum of two

What modern society (and working culture) hasn't quite caught up with is the fact that working mothers are actually the opposite of the distracted baby-brain reluctant employees that we suppose them to be. Yes, working mothers might be late occasionally and have to respond to external factors whisking them out of the office early more than the average childless worker, but working mothers are in fact arguably the most passionate, focused, cut-the-crap-and-get-to-the-nub members of the workforce.

Until this is fully realised and facilitated by working practices – and until the Marissa Mayers (CEO of Yahoo) of the corporate world set a less supermum example by taking more than two weeks' maternity leave themselves – working mums will continue to be the great travesty of untapped talent falling by the wayside, as a sustainable working–family balance is so hard to find. Too often women trade flexibility for work that falls far below their skills and experience. So we need to continue to shout about the fact that we want to work *and* we want to mother.

The working mum's lot

Perhaps when you returned to work after having your first child the inspiring parts of your role had been sidelined 'because we know you have to get back to the baby'; maybe work simply doesn't have the same interest for you anymore; or perhaps you've had to rule out the impromptu drinks after work, which means that you aren't really in the game for promotions and essential step-up office connections.

You may feel anxious that your maternity-leave replacement was much better than you, and re-enter the workplace with your confidence trailing behind you like a reluctant toddler. But gradually you settle into a workable routine and – whisper it – not even always miss your child. Rediscover your love of lipstick and a relaxed latte. But, unless you're one of the few lucky enough to have a passion-driven can't-imagine-not-doing-it job and are paid enough to afford an enviable support structure, the arrival of any more children often marks the point when working full time stops making as much financial, logistical or emotional sense, and instead begins to deplete us of all emotional and physical resources.

We want to be there for our children enough to feel like we're being a good-enough-mum (and to assuage our guilt) and still have a job that doesn't leave us in financial deficit after paying for childcare and travel (and maybe the occasional online shoe-shopping spree).

In a 2016 article, *The Sunday Times* revealed that a mother with two children at nursery needs to earn at least £40,000 a year to make any profit from going to work. A salary of £60,000 would leave her with £36 a day after deductions (childcare, travel, pension). The average woman in a full-time job earns £24,202. And yet part-time jobs simply don't exist yet in our culture without us stepping down from our previous level of clout/ability/cash. We want a job that's interesting, challenging and gives us a sense of self, separate from family life, in order to be there more fully when we *are* in family life ... but we also need to pay bills. Is this an unreal utopia?

Women's place in the professional world has been transformed over the last 50 years: we now potentially can achieve all that men can. It may seem like there has never been a better time for women in terms of opportunity and freedom, but this freedom brings with it monumental pressure, and feels like a huge wrench when we have to relinquish it once children come along. What we haven't managed so well is to transfer responsibility for some of the more 'traditional women's roles'. And this means that while we might excel at work, we'll usually pile the pressure on at home too – and that can lead to major supermum stress.

Gradually, more light is shining on the notion of gender equality, but there's still a long way to go in terms of societal norms. In the main, children rock a woman's career boat much more than a man's. Figures from the Health and Safety Executive for 2014–15 show that the number of women experiencing strain balancing a career and family is 50% *higher* than for men the same age. Some 68,000 women aged 35 to 44 in the UK are stressed at work. These statistics may not really be that shocking when you consider the fact that the working mother is usually doing much more than working and mothering.

In the younger working-mothers' generation, women under 30 still do the majority of childcare, at 45% versus 5% of men. 'Societal norms' are hard to chip away at, and the assumption is that the woman will take responsibility for home and family – the 'emotional labour' that we talked about in Chapter 1. So, if you have a baby and still want to progress with your career, it basically means juggling one extra ball and possibly being closer to dropping them all.

> '"My wife is amazing. She's really hands on. She even changes nappies. Sometimes she cooks too! I'm so lucky." The reason we have never heard any man ever say this is because no man has ever said it. Yet we still hear women speak in these terms about their partners. We say our partners are "babysitting" their own children. We are so grateful when they unload the dishwasher.'
>
> Antonia, doula, antenatal teacher and mum of three

Share the load

Part of the problem of aiming for supermumdom is that, if you're a perfectionist, you find it hard to relinquish control anywhere. If you feel you're not quite hitting your own standards, then someone else definitely bloomin' well won't. Being a working mum there is so little actual 'control' that what we do have we tend to hold on to like a small terrier would a bone.

> 'I'm torn about the idea of going back to full-time work, thinking of a thousand excuses why no one else can do school pick-up like I can. And yet I can't devote the rest of my life to piano practice and swimming lessons, I'll go nuts.'
>
> Ellen, mum of three

For a more enjoyable life, soften into the good-enough mould rather than the superhero ideal. Let your partner prove themselves – without constantly critiquing their performance. Simply say out loud that you need help. This in itself is really hard for supermums as it means admitting, if only to yourself, that you are vulnerable, which feels like a weakness – you can't do it all yourself. We complain that our partners don't help out enough, but are we actually clinging on to a 'motherhood privilege' idea that inherently we are better, by dint of being the mum? This feeling will stifle equality. To really share the load you need to relinquish the 'mama knows best' privilege, at least in part.

If you went away for a few days, what would happen? Would your partner know what time ballet is on Saturday and where the swimming kit lives? If it's not even, and you're both working, try and change it. Look for balance in the shared tasks at home: say he cooks, pays the bills and does the washing; you do all the shopping and the school runs. If necessary, see how you can shift things about to make it fair.

Undoubtedly, and increasingly, there are men out there who are feminists, who want to take up 'sharental' leave or would jump at the chance to be the full-time stay-at-home parent, who are tired of being described as 'babysitting their own children' … and are still not being talked to in equal parental terms in antenatal services, at playgroups, in their workplace, etc. It is going to involve a seismic shift across the genders for men and women to be truly equal. But by seeing it as *everyone's* issue and not just a 'mum issue', we can start making a difference.

Reconsider the load

At times when you feel overwhelmed, and anxiety starts to pay you daily visits, take a deep breath and a very clear objective look at how you use your time. Laura Vanderkam, in her book *I Know How She Does It*, raises an interesting idea that perhaps we're not actually as crazy busy as we *think* we are.

She took a sample of working women and asked them to diarise a working week. The sample group were high achievers, high earners with at least one child at home. Vanderkam asked them to accurately log their activities for 168 hours of the week. What she discovered was that these women averaged a pretty typical 40-hour week, even though they all estimated that they worked much longer hours. They felt tired, but actually on average had all slept around 7.7 hours per night – actually quite a decent night's kip!

Why not try this: keep a log in your notebook or on your phone for a full week, detailing exactly how much time you spend at work, being honest about how much of that time is *actually* stressful, and how much you are stressing about as an idea. Our *thoughts* about stress and tiredness are making us more anxious.

But, what if you're not *actually* as tired and stressed as you *think you are*? In order to calm your anxious bristling cat down, look objectively at how your time is spent. Breathe. Review your week in black and white on the page, and then, with that in front of you, consider if there are any areas that *do* need to change, and how you could do this.

Your dominant story

Narrative therapy is a useful therapy to delve into in order to unlock your relationship to your working life and your choices about being a working mother (or reconciling yourself to qualms about *not* being a working mother). Narrative therapy seeks to find patterns in stories, to uncover particular ways of understanding people's identities or understanding problems and their effects.

We all have 'stories'. I'm sure you can conjure a few of your best life stories if you close your eyes for a minute: stories about who we are, our biggest struggles, big life events, relationships, failures, wins. What's your bestseller? We naturally impose an omnipotent authorial role in our life by linking certain events together in a particular sequence, as a way to make sense of them. We invest meaning in our experiences constantly, weaving a thread through the events to form our different stories. We become so attached to our story that we might forget that we can choose to evolve the story and write a new chapter any time.

You might have a dominant story about yourself as a 'career woman', as being successful and competent, being defined and crystallised by your job title – it is 'who you are'. All the events in your life plot so far tie in with this dominant story in your life, and it has a profound effect on your life, shaping it for the future. You may have felt balanced and in control of this narrative. And, let's face it, first time around we were all beautifully naïve about the way children would affect our working personas and dreams, weren't we? They would just slot in seamlessly to the dominant narrative, not disrupt the story at all.

> 'I was very much a professional career woman and supremely uninterested in babies. I felt devastated on my last day of work before starting my maternity leave.'
>
> Victoria, mum of two

So when another narrative strand of motherhood is introduced, it can feel profoundly confusing – a clash of stories, a plot twist that we haven't quite factored in – altering your role not just in your own story but in that of your relationship and community. It might feel like you're in an episode of *I Love Lucy* as you are suddenly plunged into 1950s stereotypical roles of mum stuck at home and dad going out to work to earn the bacon.

Pottering through our lives we are constantly engaged in mediating between the dominant stories and the alternative stories, the sub plots if you like, of our lives. We are always negotiating and interpreting our experiences. Narrative therapy relates not just to you, but to your role within your family, within the community. Narratives are multi-layered: you choose to place yourself in a certain story at a certain role, pivotal or responsive.

ACTIVITY

A narrative conversation

In thinking about the issues facing you in relation to your career and life now, it can be helpful first to think about what the issue is. This activity is an example of the start of a narrative conversation, aimed at externalising a problem and changing your stance in relation to it.

1. Ask yourself, 'If this problem had a name, what would it be?' It might be 'The curse of the supercareer woman' or 'The shadowy, lurking not-good-enough suspicion', or something else. Whatever it is, give it a name that is yours and means something to you.

2. Then ask yourself, 'What are the effects of this problem on my life?' and 'What has this problem got me thinking, feeling and doing?' Go into as much detail as you can: 'How does this problem affect my relationships?', '... my work?', '... other people?' It is important to remember that *you are not the problem*. The problem (whatever name you have given it) is the problem.

3. The previous step allows you to think then about how you would like to respond to the problem. Ask yourself, 'What has it been like sharing my life with "The lurking suspicion" until now?' and 'Who would I rather have in charge of my life?'

4. If you are finding yourself thinking that you would rather take control of your own life now, then ask yourself why. 'What kind of life am I interested in that is at odds with the life that "The curse" wants for me?' and 'What does this position reflect about the things that are really important to me?'

Your 'once upon a time' ...

ACTIVITY

Tap into your story-telling talents, which you might not have delved into since you were a child, to write your own story (i.e. about you).

- In your notebook, write down your career narrative as you see it: the obstacles you might have had to overcome, the highs, the lows. In this way we can see ourselves as central to our narrative momentum – actors in our own lives.

- Unpacking and reading in black and white on the page about your working story – or the choices you made that led to you deciding *not* to continue working after having children – can make you see purpose and direction in something that in your head feels a bit aimless.

- If you're feeling overwhelmed about the balance of work in your life, consider that you *have a choice* with your plot directions.

- Anxiety can prevent you from making even the smallest of choices with any kind of confidence. So, why not imagine yourself as a famous actor, and consider, in their high self-esteem and position, how they would approach this situation.

Core beliefs at work again

Many women juggle being supermum and super career woman without questioning why – whether it's sustainable or even the right thing to do. We may not have considered that we have choices, that there could be an alternative to striving for perfection in all aspects of our lives.

It can all come from the same underlying core beliefs that we've investigated in previous chapters: 'I am not good enough', 'I am not lovable', 'I am a failure' – leading to our creating a teepee of behaviours around ourselves that we believe are keeping us safe (perhaps from others ever finding this out about us – see the discussion about imposter syndrome, below and on page 49) but are actually trapping us within a self-fulfilling cycle, which is unsustainable.

More importantly, juggling it all and striving for perfection can prevent us from reaching out and admitting that we're struggling. That act in itself can release some anxiety about things and make it more bearable. So: if you do nothing else as a result of this chapter, maybe call your best friend and say that you're finding it hard.

Imposter syndrome

Imposter syndrome: those master criminal high-achieving individuals who suffer a persistent fear of being exposed as a 'fraud'. Proof of success is dismissed as luck, timing, or as a result of deceiving others into thinking they are more competent than they 'actually are'. Imposter syndrome is particularly common among high-achieving women who view 'perfect' as the only legitimate benchmark, and if you couple that with lack of confidence often associated with returning to work post-kids/feeling guilty that your child keeps getting sick and making you look flaky at work, it's an anxious mixture.

This is where we need to work on our self-belief. You're not alone in the imposter camp. There are many, many successful women there to keep you company: Facebook's chief operating officer, Sheryl Sandberg, is author of *Lean In*, which is a book about the balancing act of parenting versus working, as well as myriad challenges of 'blatant and subtle sexism, discrimination and sexual harassment' women face while trying to thrive in a male-dominated work culture. She has said, 'there are still days when I wake up feeling like a fraud, not sure I should be where I am.' Many other highly successful women in business and the world of entertainment have admitted they also succumb to the inner voice of doubt.

Think back to our discussion of Transactional Analysis (page 157). What would it take for you to be Adult, rather than descending into your self-critical Parent (this role most likely stems from the critical messages your parents gave you) or criticised Child, at work?

Is it a question of your posture – what about checking in with your Wonder Woman stance (see page 107) in the loos at the beginning of the day?

Listen to your internal dialogue when it comes to work: are you allowing automatic thoughts to sabotage your spirit? Are you thinking, 'I'm not good enough', 'I can't do this', 'They must think I'm not committed as I have to leave at 4.30p.m. every day', as your monkey mind leaps from branch to branch in the negative tree? Imagine the potential you would unlock if you dwelled on the positive as much as you do on the negative, and challenged the negative thoughts also by reminding yourself that 'I am good enough', 'It is OK to leave the office at 4.30p.m.', 'I work hard all the time I am here', 'I am also a great mum.'

Compliment log

ACTIVITY

In your notebook, make a list of the things you do well at work.

- Write down the skills and attributes that, in your own opinion, are your professional merits.
- Also record the compliments that colleagues have given you.
- Write down a good thing that happened at work every day for a week. After a period of committing to doing this, you might notice that you are creating a *habit* of seeking the positive and are less compounded by negative thoughts at work or about your working routine, and are becoming more confident and assertive at work as a direct result of this.

- *Focus on the good* – flip your thinking around to seek out only positivity, and see how this is like fixing a confidence puncture.

The system of 360-degree feedback in the workplace is gaining momentum, and you could use this to get some accurate positive feedback on your performance. Ask colleagues some powerful questions, directly or via email, including:

- 'When I am working at my best, what are the things I do well that you most value?' or

- 'Which one thing that I do well would you like me to do even more of?'

If a whole workplace asked each other these questions, imagine the results!

ACTIVITY

Bringing your own brass band

This activity is about really singing your own praises.

- Imagine that you are surrounded by your own brass band, and that each instrument is there to celebrate your body of work, the skills and qualities that you bring to your work, and, if you like, to other aspects of your life: mothering, relationships.

- Either visually drawing as cartoons or sketches, or in written form, take some time to visualise and list the particular strengths, talents and resources that you think you have.

- You might even imagine your own signature tune – what is it that makes your band and your music unique to you?

- Imagine others standing round while the whole band celebrates your achievements.

- Be proud.

The grass is always greener

The financial pressure is on and you have to return to work. Your work has basically told you it's full time or no time. Or, you love your job but feel split in two, and are scared of even considering taking a career break in case the drawbridge comes up and you never get back in. However it comes about, if you *have* to go back to work you can begin to resent the 'luxury' of stay-at-home mums – being 'kept women', the time they get to spend with their children (which you imagine is lovingly filled with patience and craft-based activities), their ability to go to yoga or drink prosecco at any time of day.

I work as a Pilates teacher, and a freelance writer and editor. I work from home, the majority of the time. It means I am always able to pick up my son from school, and hopefully be there for all assemblies, on hand for any A&E trips due to school-playground stick-combat-related incidents (deep sigh) ... the holy grail of flexible working? Work that truly works? Well, yes, indeed ... perhaps. But I'd be lying if I claimed I didn't occasionally gaze with envy at those school-run mums who drop their child and whizz off to make their commuter train on time, lipstick at the ready for a whole day in the adult world of coffee and meetings. Grass is greener syndrome is a real bitch.

There's a mum on my school run who always looks uber glamorous in her running gear every morning. I have created a fictional life for her in which she spends her days exercising at her leisure, then lunches in an Instagram-worthy establishment, then swans around shopping/meeting friends/generally being fabulous all afternoon and never having to worry about deadlines, invoicing, brain-numbing spreadsheets. I am envious of the life that I have created for her. I've never actually spoken to her.

Envy about others (especially when they have an element of fantasy like this) is an interesting flag to unpick a little to help us understand a bit more about ourselves. This could highlight something really useful about the way you are choosing to live life, and maybe even allow you to have a lightbulb moment about changes you may wish to make.

ACTIVITY

Harness the green-eyed monster

Take a few minutes to reflect on the mums at school or work who stand out to you.

- Think particularly about those who evoke strong feelings of envy.
- Spend some time trying to consider why this might be.
- Try to get to the *assumptions* that you are making about these mums. You may be making assumptions about their lifestyle, their parenting or about them as individuals.
- Then, think about why that aspect (of their life, parenting or them) is so important to *you*. It may be because they are highlighting parts of a lifestyle you want, or that they have qualities that you would like to show more of.
- Try to think about how you can use this new knowledge to make a small change to leave you feeling more satisfied.

Sometimes, even just acknowledging that you feel envy is enough to shift your energy to make a positive change.

ACTIVITY

Compared to me

We're so used to comparing ourselves to others and judging ourselves harshly. Why not turn this around and compare yourself to yourself?

- Sit down and allow yourself at least five minutes to write down in your notebook a list of achievements that you've made in the past year.
- It can be a flowing paragraph rather than a list, or even a poem, a collection of words, doodles.
- Write whatever comes into your mind as a way of celebrating your achievements, and make sure you write for the full five minutes.
- Personal, professional – whatever comes to mind. Tiny and grand.
- Take some time to read over your achievements.

This activity will allow you to feel gratitude for developments that you've made, positive habits you've created, that you might not have even noticed. You'll see in black and white how you've overcome challenges and tricky situations, and the things you've done with your kids that have resonated.

It's a way of building a sense of appreciation for yourself, fostering kindness rather than self-deprecation. Whenever you feel your internal dialogue rerouting towards self-criticism in the form of comparison to someone who is 'better' than you, or feeling that you are not coping, come back to this activity.

Overwhelmed with choice

Maybe you don't particularly love your job but you love the freedom and the unshackled buggy-free feeling. But you can't shake the guilt that comes with 'abandoning' your children and being a 'selfish career woman'. Because you've made a choice, you question what you are doing all of this for. If you *have* to work to bring the money in, this almost takes away the emotion and conflict in your heart as there is no choice – which is easier than having a choice and then feeling guilty. Sometimes having a *choice* makes it worse, as we then use it as a stick to beat ourselves with.

'I'm currently rushing out the door to do the nursery then school drop-off, then rushing to work where I'm the last one in then first one out, and feeling like I'm pretty much fucking everything up because I then get the kids home and it's nearly 7p.m. and they're all knackered and melt down at bedtime and ...
BREATHE. I am constantly trying to decide whether any of this is worth it – but terrified of not working because hubby is in sales – there's no compromise on family-friendly, flexible hours for my other half. Right now, I think being a stay-at-home mum would benefit us all. It's a constant merry-go-round in my head. My husband is away a lot for work. The kids need the stability of me being here. They hate when he's away. And I really hate all the rushing. But despite his level, his wage is still not really that much to support a family of five. It's a daily battle I like to have with myself.'

Charlotte, mum of three

Although being able to make decisions and choices is a healthier place to be than not being able to make them, it can also mean us taking complete responsibility for all the decisions we make and therefore heaping on the guilt in spades.

When weighing up a choice, it is worth remembering that decisions can be changed, there is rarely one final one, that they are constantly reviewed. As a parent, *you make the best decision with all the information you have at the time.* As other things change or come to light, you adapt. Your choices might change.

Try to see your situation as a flowing river to sail along rather than as a block of stone to climb: if you meet obstacles, changes of direction, you will bend and change according to the change in circumstance or demands. Even though decisions about work *feel* finite, *they are not.* You do have the power to change things if you have to. This can help bring an acceptance to your situation – your and your child's situation is 'good enough.'

> *'I went back to my job as a primary school teacher when my first son was seven months old. The pain of leaving him was actually physical. I ached to my core. It felt all wrong, frustration, helplessness. So over time I have shifted and edited, and now finally have a work/life balance that I'm really happy with. I'm a working mum – but not, as far as my children were concerned. Being self-employed is annoying. I don't make much money. I have to do tax returns. I have to chase people up and stay on top of admin. But being self-employed is also absolutely wonderful. I'm free.'*
> Antonia, doula, antenatal teacher and mum of three

Antonia made the choice that she wanted to rearrange the pieces of her life puzzle to create a picture that worked better for her and her family, to allow her the joint freedom of being able to work, but not at the expense of being a mother. At the heart of narrative therapy, as we saw on page 185, is the understanding that 'the problem is the problem' and that we have a *relationship* with it. This means that we can change how we respond to it.

If we are 'actors in our own lives', then our actions are within our control *and are ours to choose.* This idea of 'being free' is so important in terms of our emotional health. It isn't always about the choices we make, but the idea that *we can choose to make them*, which feels liberating.

Staying emotionally healthy

Being able to make decisions is important – especially if you are at a time in your life when it feels like things are out of control and overwhelming. Sometimes making decisions about small day-to-day things can help you slowly regain a sense of mastery.

- If someone asks you how you take a cup of tea or what you would like to watch on TV, make a choice and verbalise it. *Don't say, 'I don't mind'*.

- Even if you don't particularly care about what you are being asked to choose (and if life feels overwhelming it may well be that you don't), make a decision anyway.

- Make a point of telling yourself if you are the one making tea or watching TV.

- Conscious decision making can really help give you back your sense of control.

Making small daily decisions such as deciding to commit to a walk every lunch break to calm your mind will begin to lift you out of anxiety-induced inaction and fear.

Wheel of life

This is a life-coaching activity for gaining a fresh perspective on the areas of your life that are getting you down and *not* in balance. It gives you a visual guide to how you're feeling overall in life, but also breaks down where you might be feeling particularly low or depleted. It may highlight something that you weren't even aware of.

It's essentially a basic circle, divided into segments – usually eight, but feel free to make it ten if you feel there are areas appropriate to your life that aren't featured in the example.

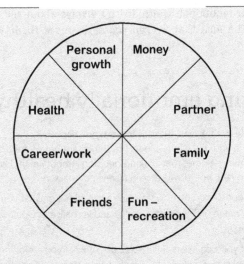

Figure 2. The Wheel of Life

Each section of the pie has a rating scale of 1–10, representing how you're doing right now – 1 being the lowest, 10 the highest. After you rate each segment, you mark out your scores, then connect the dots. In the end, you get a web-like diagram that gives you an instant idea of how you're doing.

It's hard to know how you are doing in your overall life when you're so focused on the daily grind of school runs and steel-band practice. The wheel shows whether you are actually noticing all the areas that might be crying out for attention – e.g. if you feel you'd rate your relationships (friendships, not just your partner relationships) as a 3, you might have a lightbulb moment that you need to prioritise some time catching up with friends. Look at ways that you could change how you feel about any 'low' areas.

It can invite a real epiphany, noticing that there are areas getting you down that you hadn't considered – and also seeing that some areas are working well. Please note though that an 'ideal' life is not necessarily one where every aspect is a 10 – we need to be realistic! We are striving for a better balance, not the perfect life.

Before you start this exercise, maybe write the date on your wheel so you can do it again at regular two- or three-monthly intervals and compare the result with previous efforts; this will allow you to have a true look at your progress.

Vision boarding

In a similar way, you can use a visual guide to create the type of balance that you want in the future: visualising it means you will be able to bring yourself closer to that goal. It's also fun to get stuck in with scissors and magazines, hunting for images to pin to a cork board, or glue to a sheet of card, a 3-D Pinterest!

- Have a look for images relating to your working/family life that appeal to you – words, pictures, affirmations.

- What sparks joy for you, makes you feel positive, determined, focused?

- What is the ideal mixture for you of working and family life?

- What would your ideal work balance/workspace/job actually look like? For example, are you drawn mainly towards images of palm trees and hammocks? Could this be a very simple way of your brain telling you that you need to take a break?

- How could you manifest this in a small and real way in your daily life? Breathing? Mindfulness? Yoga?

Assembling images of your 'ideal' may shift your mindset and unlock things that you hadn't considered being achievable. And vision boarding is proven to make you more positive about putting behaviours in place that help you work towards intended action when you have a visual impetus there to spur you on.

The process of this will be interesting in itself. If you can clearly see that you have an unrealistic vision board, this can suggest that you are striving to be a 'supermum'.

Letting go of guilt

Sarah is a mum of two who has just gone back to work full time after having her second baby. 'I battle daily over mum woes/guilt. My children's nursery workers see my children far more than I do. They mother them more than me! I have to take their word for it when they tell me what my baby likes to do, her quirks and traits, as those rushed weekends of being with her, my toddler and my husband just don't ever really compensate for not spending 8a.m.–7p.m. with them, Monday–Friday.

'The transition from a year's maternity leave where I didn't leave my first baby's side for the entire year, to having not spent one whole day alone with him for two YEARS when I went on maternity leave again was bonkers. When I had my second, I just had no clue what the hell to do with a three-year-old. I've always found myself at ease with babies but the reality of spending this extra time with a fully fledged three-year-old little personality I should embrace and be grateful for. Yet there were many days I ended up texting a stream of angry impatience to the husband when he pushed my limits too far. And now I feel guilty that yet again he's into full-time childcare, along with his little baby sister.

'So for me it's a constant rollercoaster of trying to balance full-time working mum guilt to then wanting to hide in a cupboard for some peace when I DO get to be with my children. I never feel I'm doing a good enough job. I'm not a "crafty" mum, I'm impatient and lazy. And I LOVE MY SLEEP so it sometimes makes me feel venomous towards my children that they steal it from me!'

Working full time can bring with it a huge amount of guilt for imposing your schedule onto your child, particularly if they're small. Neshe, who has a five-year-old and works full time, explains, 'my son always says that he hates the after-school club. It makes me feel awful. I pick him up at 6p.m., and it *is* a long day, for both of us. We're both so tired. And so I don't give him the energy and attention that he needs at the end of the day. I always say "OK, stop now, that's enough", and then I feel guilty. It makes me feel that I'm not doing a very good job as a mum.'

Taking time to clear your mind, to offer a delineated space between work you and mum you, is important here in order to feel like you're not short-changing your child (and yourself) in these moments.

After work, before you pick your child up, take a few moments to breathe, soften, do a mindful scan of your body. Choose one of the breathing or mindfulness activities that we have already worked on in the book – see page 108, for example.

If you feel like you 'don't have time' to do this as you're constantly at full pelt, *it's even more important that you do it*. If you can pause and therefore be more present, less frazzled when you reconnect with your child at the end of the day, that's a bonus for both of you. One minute is all you need: time actually elongates when you slow down and allow it to – and you really *do* have a minute to spare.

> 'Women who work aren't evil, just as stay-at-home mums aren't lazy. There is a happy medium. I try and accept "good enough" as a mum but it's mainly that I know now after three kids that there simply isn't a Right Way. I think the key is to know yourself, respond to your child, and avoid guilt as it's a pointless emotion.'
>
> Jessica, mum of three

Let's take another look at what we explored in Chapter 1. Guilt organises responses related to a violation of values. It focuses us on actions and behaviours that hope to repair the violation.

As mums we tend to fall into the supermum trap of paying too much attention to what other people say/think and not looking within to see whether we trust our own choices. Guilt is associated with 'should/ must' type thoughts. 'I should be spending more time with my kids', 'he should be sleeping through the night.' We have to revisit the fact that motherhood is not a competition. It's not one big sports day where we'll get a rosette if we're the winner. It's about getting through every day in a trial-and-error obstacle course of whatever works best for your family.

Guilt is often one of the 'stories' we tell ourselves. We frame our guilt story negatively. 'Threaten-to-swallow-me-whole guilt' might be the name of one of the problems that has come into your life since going back to work. Guilt may invite you to think that you are stunting your child's emotional growth, or that you are abandoning them by putting them in after-school club.

Guilt may invite you also to act in certain ways, to 'make up for everything'. Your choice is then how to respond to guilt's invitations. In asking yourself, 'What does guilt want my life to look like?' versus 'What do I want my life to look like?', you might have a clearer idea about whether you need to ignore guilt and/or make some decisions to feel, think or act differently.

We need to either act on the guilt, take stock and work out whether your child is genuinely struggling and whether you need to find a solution, or ignore it. If you are moving life in the direction that you want it to go, then think about how you should position yourself in relation to guilt. Instead of accepting guilt's invitations, question its intentions and assert yourself.

For example, you can choose to embrace after-school club for its many positives. When you hear guilt's voice, remind yourself about the skills you are affording your child by allowing them to go to after-school club: making friends, learning new things. Tell them (and yourself) how well they are (and you are) doing. Recognise it, value it, celebrate it and build on it. Find the positive.

The world is full of differing opinions on motherhood: 'Oh, you're going back to work *already?*' and 'So, did you decide not to go back to work then? *Lucky you!*' being offered in tandem by society as a way of slapping you whichever way you turn. Guilt if you miss your child. Guilt if you don't miss your child. Unless you're prepared to alter the course of your life to make up for this, it is not purposeful guilt and you simply need to shed it. Wear your own mothering choices with confidence.

ACTIVITY

Ditch the guilt

Write a list

- Write down everything you feel guilty about.
- Review your list. Is it all based in reality?
- Have you created a guilt story in your mind?
- Are you basing your guilt on someone else's comments or opinion?

Personify your guilt

- Give your guilt a name and a character of its own.
- Think about its story – when did it first show up and what are some of the ways it has tried to influence your life?

- How has it grown over time, and how might you have inadvertently fed it?

- Have there been ways that you have felt tricked or hoodwinked by Guilt into doing things you did not want to?

- Think about some ways you might try to reduce the influence that Guilt has on your life.

- How could you turn its voice down and make more of your own choices?

Take action

- If you feel as if your full guilt list is insurmountable, take *one* guilt source and see if there is even a small thing you can do to make it better.

- For example: do you feel you never have the energy to play with your child, or read with them at the end of a tiring work day? Well, OK, then *make the time*. Schedule it in – cancel something else from the to-do list if necessary, and make it happen.

- See if that assuages the guilt. If it does, commit to doing it regularly.

Journaling

- In your notebook, write yourself a positive parenting journal.

- Each day, write down something that you want to remember/celebrate about what you did that day.

Developing resilience

Resilience is that ineffable quality that acts as a lifejacket to keep us afloat when sailing in choppy waters. To a certain extent, we need to throw life's 'stuff' at our children – it gives them a good grounding in the world and teaches them how to develop the resilience they will need to face difficult things: we can't protect them from experiencing the real world.

There are a few factors that help to make someone resilient. As we have seen in the activities up to now, both a positive attitude and optimism can be developed through training and practice in order to build your resilience reserves. A resilient person is in tune with and able to manage emotions, to learn from 'failures' and to reframe experiences positively.

If you're feeling emotionally turbulent about your day-to-day patterns and routines, make sure you take some time to check in with your children's behaviour, with this in mind. Are they showing signs of being angry, frustrated, sad, confused? If so, are they *reflecting how you feel* in any way? Being aware of your own feelings and what might be eliciting them is the first step, and sometimes a useful one, in trying to understand what might be going on inside your child's mind.

Emotional regulation

If a young person feels out of control and distressed, the last thing they need is an adult who sees their high display of emotion and raises them an extra dollop of anxiety. Emotions are powerful and if we're not aware of them they can drive our actions in an unthinking way.

With mindfulness, and with the 'thought-police' tools that we've been developing over the course of this book, we can develop the capacity to use the rational parts of our brain to regulate our emotions – to smooth them out a bit. And the more we can model that for children (and maybe even for that particularly tetchy colleague), the more it will help them to cope with life's crumpled bits too. It's OK and completely normal to feel anxious, upset or angry at times – acknowledging this can be helpful in itself, for all of us. Vocalising when things might be feeling tricky, and asking for help, should be seen as a sign of strength, not weakness.

For the under threes, how we approach our family set-up is laying the foundations for their lifetime's character and core beliefs – so we need to balance working with trying our best to find the right childcare solution for their wellbeing. Teenagers probably have days when they'd rather you weren't around quite so much, and the best mother–teen relationships may thrive on quality rather than quantity when it comes to time spent together – the perfect time to start to reignite a career flame, perhaps.

A 2015 study conducted by the University of Harvard, using data from 24 countries including the UK and US, revealed that while working mothers 'often internalise social messages of impending doom for their children', the reality is that their sons and daughters appear to thrive, with daughters benefiting most from the positive role model of a mother with a career. If you choose to work, you *have* to stop wrangling internally about whether it's the right thing – unless you are actually going to do anything about it.

Flex appeal: work that works

Since 2003, the right to request flexible working (and have employers give this proper consideration) has been enshrined in law for parents of children under 16. Men and women are increasingly searching for the blend of challenge and flexibility *and remuneration* that truly flexible working should offer. But until flexible working options complement rather than clash with the higher status, well-paid echelons of working life, priorities will continue to be career development and salary rather than speaking out about flex.

> 'When I announced my second pregnancy at work I was treated nearly with disdain. I wasn't told about meetings because they thought I couldn't make them due to childcare commitments, I was not invited on work trips for unknown reasons. I asked for some additional training in a few key areas but my request kept getting put off and the funds for the course deemed too high, or the time out of the office too long. This was despite other people going on courses in the same team. I think it all boiled down to them thinking I'd definitely never come back once I'd had my second child. Pretty depressing really.'
>
> Tanya, mum of two

> 'I did try to go back to working full time. But I realised that my image of myself wasn't this super career woman any more but that I just wanted to be a good mum. Maybe this is sad and the wrong thing to say nowadays? My son once said to me that they were asked at school what it meant to be a good mother, and he said "always at home and doing everything for you" … it made me really angry because they weren't even asked what makes a good father.'
>
> Josie, mum of two

Nearly 70% of mothers in the UK work. There are now as many working mothers as working women without children. No surprise then that enabling and retaining the talents of the 'working mother' is a huge social, cultural, political and economic issue. The glossy shine of supermum syndrome is starting to look tarnished, as we have begun to see that women shouldn't aim to 'have it all' if that means being too bloomin' knackered to appreciate any of it.

> 'I'm totally "unemployable", in the traditional sense. My ideal is a job that's 9–3, that is flexible around school holidays, where I can take time off for inset days, school plays and assemblies, that challenges me and inspires me. I'm basically unemployable so I decided to employ myself.'
>
> Becks, mum of two and small-business owner

If you need inspiration for flexible working and how it can work and be integrated into a fully functioning society, just look for pictures of the Italian MEP Licia Ronzulli, who has taken her daughter into parliament from when she was a newborn, breastfed her in front of the eyes of the world, shown her that a woman is strong and has a voice to be heard. Working life does not have to stop when you have a baby. The more present and accepted we can make this image, the less guilt we will be made to feel when we choose to work. We just have to make peace with the various jigging arounds that we have to do in order to make it work.

Giving up work to be a SAHM (Stay-at-Home Mum)

Maybe the cost of childcare prohibits your return to work, or you've just done some maths and realise that you really want to put your children before your career, for a while. Giving up work to mother full time may be a lot of women's dreams. But is it the Elysian Fields that we might imagine it to be? If you've been independent and made your own money up until that point in your life, it can feel like a real shift in power within your relationship. It might mean complete financial dependence on your partner, and that can have a real effect on the emotional balance between the two of you.

'My husband works in the City and so he earns a lot, way more than I ever did in my job in publishing. Because I wasn't really earning much, we decided that he would "do the money" and I would "do the children". But this means that now I feel annoyed if he starts stepping on my toes with parenting decisions. And I occasionally miss my old life where I was confident and heard in the adult world. I love being with my kids, but it has been a challenging choice.'

Rachel, mum of three

'Staying at home with a teething baby is hard. Despite playgroups and playgrounds, the hours stretch out in front of you, and you feel lonely and bored, and then guilty for feeling lonely and bored because you should be savouring all of the moments. But each moment has you wondering where the woman you were has gone.'

Antonia, doula, antenatal teacher and mum of three

You might be made to feel crappy by barbed comments about how 'lucky' you are, made by working mothers who are feeling guilty and frazzled by their own situation. You might simply wonder why it is that there is no status conferred upon mothers – why is raising the future seen as such a lowly profession, when surely it's among the most extraordinary and important?

'I went out for drinks with an old friend and her workmates. She introduced me to the group saying, "This is Nikki, she stays at home with her children but she used to be a top lawyer" ... and I thought, well, why not just say she's a mum, rather than trying to boost my status by saying what I "used to" be. Just get over it. I'm a mum at home with my kids, I'm fine with that.'

Nikki, mum of two

Under these circumstances, it can be helpful to shift yourself to a more powerful position where you *choose to respond* rather than are *made to feel*. It's your life and your choice. Allow other's thoughtless comments and judgements be theirs. Flick them off like fluff on your coat.

Finding peace

If more often than not you are feeling out of kilter, feeling like you're missing out on your children and there is no balance, you need to take a good look at your choices and see if you can re-evaluate. Look at what success means to you. Look at whether you are asking too much of yourself.

You only have one life. Your children are only dependent on you for a short time (OK, so maybe there's a chance nowadays they will still be living with you when they're 35, but that's for another book ...). There *will* be time to pick up and recharge your career at a later point in time, if you can financially withstand pressing pause right now. But there won't be another time when your kids are at school.

Striving for perfection isn't a great example or legacy for our children. As psychologist Donald Winnicott said, the best mother is the good-enough mother (see page 137). 'Muddling through' imperfectly might be the answer, with some days having more supermum wins than others. Our children need us to be present in heart and body, whenever we are with them. If you're wracked with guilt, questioning your choices and feeling crappy, you are not fully with them.

Case study: Flexing around children

Estelle, a nurse and mum of two, took a step back from her career in favour of her children. It can often feel like you're stuck in the mud if your career takes a back seat while your kids are small. But this can be a breathing space, a breeding ground for the future when there is more time, space and commitment to be given. Your career can thrive and flourish – you might just have to have some patience to see it unfurling.

'It is so frustrating being a mum, whatever choices you make, particularly around work.

'On the one hand I wanted to be with my boys full time but, oh how that did my head in at times! I was lucky – working in a shift-work setting I had the option to work part time. However, nothing is easy! In my job you can pretty much decide your hours, as in how many, but not when you work. So the trade-off for me was that I did a month of days then a month of nights alternating, two 12-hour shifts per week.

'Working 12 hours with little sleep, less so on nights, was tough to put it mildly. At times it was great – I felt I still had a bit of "me". But on the flip side I missed weekends and family events; my second son's first Christmas was clouded by the thought of going to work overnight – I had to work over Christmas so I picked that shift so it minimised the impact on everyone else, but I knew work was in the background *all the time.*

'My husband is great in terms of childcare and support, but it always fell to me to get the shifts and organise who was where when; he always did his fair share but didn't have the stress of coordinating it all.

'Before kids I had a secondment to a more senior position, which coincided with having kids. In a way it suited me as I was able to take a step back and be part time, but in ways that was frustrating because I knew I had the potential to give and be so much more professionally but working part time meant I was stuck at the top of my band with nowhere to go. But I kept on moving forward, providing professional and high standards of care, knowing my time would come. This year with my boys both in school I have a new job, still part time, but I am able to attend more meetings and be more flexible in school hours – I am now working in a specialist role and moving on in my career. It is really very satisfying.

'When your kids are little, taking a step back career wise might feel frustrating/soul destroying/static/unfulfilling but actually being a mummy to small children is time you will never get back and there will always be other career opportunities.

'We will be working until we are 70ish – is a few static years in your job going to kill your career? No! Even though it feels like that at times. Plus, cuddles with my boys far outweighs any job satisfaction.

Basically if you have small children and a career, now might not be your time – and that is ok!'

Ditch the guilt, calm your anxiety and find peace with your choices. There are 24 hours in the day, and there is one you. There is no perfect work–life balance, just as there are no perfect parents – there is only good enough. You are trying your best to get it right, and that in itself is good enough. If you can't find peace with your current situation, make a plan and, step by step, rearrange the pieces of the puzzle to begin to build a different picture, in which you are living the life that feels *right* for you and your family.

8

Have more joy: finding positive in the day to day

This chapter is all about injecting more joy and playfulness into the day to day, and allowing yourself to feel a bit lighter and brighter. Through the activities in this book you've learnt to disrupt your negative thinking and dismantle the anxiousness that leads to feelings of inadequacy; it's time to rebuild your confidence by finding your smile, focusing on the things that make you happy, and simply remembering to enjoy your children and your life.

Maybe you're worrying about whether your child is losing their joy, their spark, their childhood, because of school pressures. Maybe you're worrying that you don't have enough to give them, after work and other demands. Fun and laughter could not be further down your list most days. All this worry means you feel you're cracking under the strain.

This chapter will help you see that those cracks are where the light shines in. If you're stuck in survival mode, it's hard to squeeze joy in when you're just trying to get through the days without losing it. Finding joy regularly will build confidence in your mum skills – laughter is the best medicine – and foster a feel-good bond with your child, which will lighten even the toughest of days.

'Tell me, what is it you plan to do with your one wild and
precious life?'

Mary Oliver, *The Summer Day*

Remember – you only get one life, so live it as joyously as you can. If we
view life as 'wild and precious', as a gift rather than a given, we can
occasionally try to change our perspective – aim to reap as much
pleasure as possible from *moments* rather than trudging through them
drearily as if it were Groundhog Day.

Life is *not* about expecting to be happy *all the time*. This quest in itself
can make us miserable because it is a completely unattainable goal.
You might feel you're failing because you're experiencing highs and
corresponding lows, rather than consistently smiling like Topsy and
Tim's inanely positive mum, but the opposite is the case. Life is multi-
layered, multi-faceted, multi-coloured – like a rainbow from dark to
light – and this means encompassing all ends of the emotional
spectrum, *in balance*.

An experience of darkness will enable light to shine brighter. Being
able to recognise and appreciate joy in the small moments every day,
truly noticing and savouring moments of pure happiness while you
experience them, will foster a more optimistic spirit overall.

Mindfulness is a key therapy in this chapter – not just in terms of its
calming benefits but as a pathway to finding 'joy' in the everyday
activities that we all as parents have to engage in: walking about with
our children, playing in the park, preparing and eating meals, spending
time at home. Let's find ways of sparking joy within this humdrum.

By being fully present with your child, which you can do even during
the most unremarkable of everyday activities, you will build a deep,
reciprocal and positive connection that will help to see you through
tricky times – those long afternoons when they're pushing your
buttons, refusing to eat their lovingly prepared dinner, and generally
making you want to ship them off to New Zealand on the next available boat.

Playtime

Picasso once said, 'Every child is an artist. The problem is how to remain an artist after he grows up.' Let's face it, children are bonkers. Sometimes this delights us. But when we're tired or have somewhere to be, it can be wearing. Children give us licence to look at things from a different perspective, literally viewing life from a different level to our own eye level. If we could harness that bonkers, artistic delight, we could unlock a new imaginative, joyful potential in the world. The world of rainbows and unicorns, snow days, fire engines, trains, bees on lavender. Pigeons. Snails. The magic of the mundane, of bus rides, playgrounds, puddles and jumping.

What can we learn from the way our children feel, think and do? If we look to them, they could help us to 'release our inner toddler'. There are lots of things you can do to tap into your inner child and recalibrate your joy barometer. As adults we take life and ourselves incredibly seriously. Maybe we need to try to lose some of the serious heaviness of being adult occasionally, be spontaneous, ask more questions, generally be more chaotic, less buttoned up.

> 'I feel like I don't laugh any more, laughter that reaches beyond my mouth I mean. My laughter doesn't travel to my eyes, my cheeks and my belly any more. I feel like "fun" has somehow escaped my life now that I've got three kids – it's all about schedules.'
>
> Bella, mum of three

Shake off your cool

As the old adage goes: 'Dance like there's nobody watching ... sing like there's nobody listening.' When children sing and dance they are truly allowing the rhythm to get them; there's no shadow of self-consciousness – it's as free as it gets. A toddler tantrum is the height of not caring what people might think. We should take a leaf out of their book and shake our cool off.

Children and inhibitions don't often go hand in hand. In order to truly thrive, to feel emotionally balanced and joyful, we adults also need to let our hair down occasionally. Whether that's getting lost in dancing, singing, running crazily like Phoebe in *Friends* – whatever it is, look at your life and see whether you have at least a small corner where you can let it all hang out and *not care what anyone thinks.*

Often it's simply about giving ourselves verification that having fun is 'enough' as a goal in itself, that we don't have more important things to do. There is a current trend of adult ball pools, adult bouncy castles, trampoline playgrounds – it's a huge growth area in the leisure industry, which suggests that grown-ups are crying out for a temporary release from the stresses of irrevocable adulthood.

If you go to softplay with your kids, do you just leave them to it, drinking a coffee and looking at your phone? Why not join them and get stuck in? My toddler is still at the age where he can't climb on his own. Going to softplay with both of my kids is brilliant – not to mention a fantastic workout with all the climbing, pushing and lifting skills required – and naturally encourages loads of laughter at the silliness of it, which is the best therapy of life. Try it.

Why not unleash your inner imaginative child, be a bit daring and overturn the rules. What's the worst that could happen? Challenge your daily grown-up habits, even down to the way you always wear your hair, the sensible black tights or non-showy earrings you always choose.

Choose to make eye contact and even (shock, horror) smile at commuters on the train. Change it up and surprise yourself a bit. Add a bit of sparkle by wearing a sequin top or starry tights to work, or a bright coral lippy on the school run instead of your normal austere nude. Embrace colour. Don't save your 'best' clothes for best, just wear what you love to wear and what makes you feel happy. Why the hell not?

Ask questions the way that children ask questions, be genuinely inquisitive about the workings of the universe: What are you doing? How does that happen? Why are you doing that? As adults we tend to limit our possibilities constantly, shorten our horizons without even questioning why. Grown-up life is all about limited possibilities – 'you can't do that', 'it's not allowed', 'there are rules', 'terms and conditions apply', 'read the small print', etc.

Try to see things as if for the first time. I'm naturally risk-averse; I'm not sure why, but I constantly worry about 'getting into trouble' or doing something wrong, or wonder whether I'm *allowed* to do something. This has been very limiting as a belief system and has made me live life as if I'm always on the verge of being told off by a scary headmaster. It's only now I'm getting older that I have a more devil-may-care attitude about the rules and getting it 'right' (not talking anything illegal here though, folks) – because, well, who exactly am I worried about upsetting? If I get 'told off' then so be it – at least I tried.

ACTIVITY

What's the rush?

Children dawdle. The level of slow-motion dawdle usually appears to increase in inverse proportion to the urgency of your journey.

If you stop tutting and chivvying, you can understand that this is the most pure example of mindfulness, being fully present in the moment. Pausing to observe a stream of ants making its way across a path. Stopping to say hello to a cat sitting on a dustbin. Crouching down to fully appreciate the depth of a crack in the pavement.

- Once a week, when walking alone, allow yourself to completely drag your feet.

- *Keep your phone in your pocket* and look up. Observe the world around you. See what captures your attention.

- Look through living-room windows and imagine the lives that go on beyond them.

- Cross the road and walk, slowly, on the other side to your usual route.

- Wander and see where it takes you, in body and mind.

You might find that letting go of your usual practice of rushing allows you a clarity and change of mindset, which maybe sparks a sense of creativity, or might allow you a lightbulb moment for solving something that's been troubling you.

Slow down.

Be more toddler.

Learning about life through play

Play is good for us. It contributes to better health overall, happier relationships, creative thinking. It's a hugely important segment in the pie of a thriving life. During playtime, we lose ourselves in something purely for the purpose of flow and pleasure, as opposed to having a specific 'point' or purpose.

Listen to any playtime at a nearby primary school. What do you hear? Shouting, shrieking, laughing, joyful general-running-about mayhem. When do adults ever get a chance to make that kind of noise through sheer undiluted enjoyment? At a festival or gig, perhaps. Any other times ...? Playtime is time for freedom, absorption, improvisation, joy. It's a natural drive, an urge, a need: facilitated for children up until primary school but gradually suppressed the further up the grown-up ladder we climb.

Teenagers can become more painfully self-conscious and consider play too 'uncool'; then adults are just too busy – play seems too frivolous to spend effort creating time for. Leisure time becomes something carved out in an almost business-like way, marked with shouty, earnest goals such as 'lose weight', 'get fit'. No 'run like a crazy thing and play space rockets just for the hell of it' in sight.

Rediscovering the lost art of 'playtime' is crucial to letting the joy back into your lives. What we loved to do as a child, where we played, whether we were alone or with company. What sort of play did you love that brought you real joy? What activities could you try as an adult to emulate that level of freedom and joyfulness? Could you introduce any playfulness into your day to day, in what you wear, in how you interact with your family and friends? More music, more dancing, more silliness, more unicorns, more laughter?

Notice the good

Solution-focused therapy aims to find a solution to life's challenges by tweaking behaviour habits. Rather than probing the 'why' of the difficulty, instead it tries to see what there is that you can build on to create a more positive scenario. This therapy tries to get to the nitty-gritty workings of relationships by asking powerful questions such as: 'What does family life look like when it's going well?'; 'How can I do more of that?' It's a therapy that works towards setting ourselves some noticing tasks in our day-to-day habits and relationship patterns.

If we all *notice* when things go well – however infrequently that may be – and actively try and do more of that, this makes it more likely that things will go well more of the time. This is like imagining the drink in the half-empty cup, thinking about how good it might taste. Fun is a great place to focus on this. Ask yourself, 'What does our family do for fun?', 'What does Mum do purely for fun?' Involve your partner and children in the discussion – you might be surprised by what comes out.

ACTIVITY

Rate your life

This activity is about assessing how good or bad you feel your life is at present using a numerical scale, with the aim of helping you focus on the positives.

- Think of a 0–10 scale, where 0 is the worst that things have ever been and 10 is the very best that things could be.

- Now, on that scale, think about how things are currently and rate your present life.

- It is rare for a situation to be a 0 or a 10. Even if you have rated the current situation as a 1 or 2, this still suggests that *something* (even though it may be tiny) is positive (i.e. it's not 0).

- Ask yourself, 'What makes things a (whatever number you have given it)?'

- Then write down all of the things about your current situation that make it this number rather than a 0.

The things you identified in the last point can give you some clues as to what is working, or your strengths and resources in coping with a truly awful situation.

For example, even if you score things at a 1, which suggests they are pretty bad, it's about trying to work out what is in the gap between 0 and 1. The higher the number you have rated, the bigger the gap is for you to look into. The reason you didn't rate things as a 0 may just be that you are now reading this book – which highlights that you were able to create a space to think about the situation. You summoned up enough energy to start to read, and you may even now be thinking positively about this activity.

The focus of this exercise is to see a tiny ember glowing within a seemingly hopeless situation, and then fan this small flame by asking more about it and what it means.

After rating how the situation is now, try the follow-up activity below.

'Where on the scale would you be happy with the situation?'

ACTIVITY

Most people choose 7, 8 or 9. Be wary (Supermums!) of choosing 10. It's unrealistic and unsustainable.

- Once you have chosen where you would be happy, ask yourself, 'What would this look like?' and then, crucially, 'How would that be different from my current situation?'

- In order to enable you to think about this, it can be helpful to think about the questions, 'What does family life look like when it's going well?' and 'What gets in the way of that happening more?'

Family therapy

Can you remember a time when your own parents had fun with you, and how this made you feel? How far do you have to cast your mind back?

> *'Fun is a must in my crazy family. I have to laugh every day. We are all silly and have lots of "in" jokes. I think that strengthens our bond as a unit.'*
>
> Cee, mum of two

Reconnecting with our own family memories and childhood allows you to dip into what you did that you loved, and may delve into lost treasures such as what are your favourite memories of your own parents?

The family album

Take the opportunity to go through your own family photos.

● Pick out ones of family holidays, birthdays or special times that you associate with a sense of joy and belonging.

● Take the time to really look at these photos and remember the smells, sounds and feel of the day.

● Think about these memories.

● What was it for you as a child that made these days special?

● Imagine the memories that your children are creating.

● What kinds of sounds, smells, colours, etc. would you like their album to conjure up for them in years to come?

First-time-bump

Another way of tapping into past unfettered joy is to think back and reconnect with the hopes and dreams of parenthood you held, from before you had your children. We didn't imagine we would be running round, stressed out trying to manage a hundred different commitments, shouting 'PUT YOUR SHOES ON NOW!' at full volume. Blissfully naïve about the reality of the day-to-day mayhem, what did we really want for ourselves and our children?

The first-time-pregnant you

Find your original scan picture, if you can – or any other memorabilia, pictures, diaries, etc. that bring you back to your nearly-mum you.

● What were the qualities that you were hoping to bring to your mothering experience?

● What did you *imagine* motherhood to be like?

● Is there anything from your imaginings that you could enact, even if just for one day?

This is not to make you feel like you 'should' be aiming for your real life to be like your original imaginings – which brings us back to the origins of the supermum myth – but more that you could channel that innocent joy of first-time motherhood into your experience, even if just momentarily.

The dominant narrative of motherhood

Remembering to have joy in your daily relationship with your children is difficult. We're almost programmed against it. As Antonia, mum of three and antenatal teacher, says, 'Our culture promotes the idea that having kids is a chore. We commiserate with each other over the stresses and strains of raising our children. Motherhood is a duty we've been assigned. The fact that we actually assigned it to ourselves is forgotten. We feel sorry for ourselves. And we joke about it. We publicly yearn for bedtime and wine and shout about coffee the next morning. We blame our children for our stress levels and for our grey hairs. We all do it! But the danger of this is that these babies didn't ask to be here, we invited them.'

There is plenty of solidarity and camaraderie to be had in the 'Motherhood is Frigging Hard' camp. We *need* to share the difficulty and the frustration as it can help to flip Supermum on her head, share the vulnerability and make us aware that everyone finds it hard and we are not failing.

But how about we also attempt occasionally to challenge this dominant narrative of 'motherhood as hardship'? Could we celebrate as well as commiserate, without looking smug? High five each other at the end of a long day wrestling your children and your sanity, as you would fellow marathon runners. We've done a brilliant job!

Overscheduling

Children need lots *and lots* of unstructured playtime, time to just loll around and be bored. If your Monday–Friday is stressing you out because of ferrying your children around to ballet, tennis, music, taekwondo, swimming ... why not change it? We have an aversion to just letting our children 'be' – maybe we fear them roaming around the streets unattended, getting into mischief like kids used to in films from the '80s. But do we have to fill every spare minute? Do an audit of your week: is there anything you could strip out, to allow some down time?

If you find that in your weekly routine you feel like your children are simply one of your chores to be organised, then perhaps you need to refocus. Maybe just let them get on with things without your direction, for one afternoon a week. Go straight home from school, open the door and let everyone find their own flow. Then go and make a cup of tea, and sit down to savour the peace.

Sideways listening

Letting go of the schedule can enable unexpected spontaneous fun to creep back in, with a bit of work. Resist the urge (or the demands) to automatically put the TV on or turn on the iPad. It's so easy to rely on technology that we have forgotten that it hasn't been around forever. Just occasionally, one afternoon, see what it's like to revisit a world before Netflix. What about board games? Or one day imagine that there's a power cut – what would you do together? Making up scenarios, and generally facing activities together rather than organising for your children, enables free creative flow, is fun, and has a positive side effect of encouraging greater communication and connection between you and your kids, in the form of 'sideways listening'.

Sideways listening means literally taking away the potential self-consciousness of looking in someone's eyes, and allowing a freer flow of dialogue as a result. Good communication between parents and children is essential at every age. It's as much about listening as it is about talking (in fact maybe more so). The temptation for parents is to think we're the ones who should be doing the talking and our children should be listening. It's the *listening* you do as a parent that's the key.

Ten minutes of child-led activity every day is optimal, but aim for at least once a week if you can. Set aside a time to do whatever they want to do (within the boundaries of safety and some chaos-limiting house rules!). During this time give your full attention to your child – let them take the lead in the play and conversation: watch, wait and listen without intervening or guiding (or questioning).

Getting into a regular habit of individual, free-flowing time with your child is good to do when they are little, but will help set up a pattern that should pay huge dividends as your child grows up. It will be much easier to really listen to your teenager, and for them to know you are routinely available, if you've had this regular one-to-one listening time with them as they were growing up.

There are all sorts of enjoyable activities that lend themselves to sideways listening, such as crafty stuff, baking, running or yoga – it doesn't have to be organised or formal, dancing around the kitchen counts. Even flicking through an Argos catalogue together can be a great way of sparking off conversation and enlightening chat. Ideally make it into a habit, as your children will know that they can rely on this time with you and that it's all about them and how important they are to you.

This air of meandering, unplanned activities lends itself well to letting your children lead the conversation, with you commenting rather than questioning. This is nurturing your relationship unobtrusively rather than in a forced way, giving your child confidence to come to you and talk about anything, from all the little things that make up their day to, possibly, more worrying situations.

Recapturing your school-days

Regularly entering a school environment if your kids are at school may encourage you to remember the things you loved at school. Memories might be triggered of beloved games, or activities you had long forgotten. Think about what you loved at school and *why* you loved it (what kinds of things truly caused you happiness, flow and bliss?): music/art/PE – even something like maths homework if that's what you truly enjoyed. How can you capture the joy that maths homework gave you, in your real adult life?

Old school

Write out your week like an old school timetable, with all of your responsibilities, activities and jobs itemised in it.

Highlight in two different colours the things that give you:

1. a sense of satisfaction

2. a sense of achievement.

These things are linked to an increase in mood. So, if your timetable has little of these two colours, your general mood is likely to be low.

Try to add in at least one thing a week in each category, and work from there.

Rose tinting: What will you miss about your current family life?

Sometimes, the most effective way of appreciating the present moment is to imagine a time when it is in the past. Imagine living in your nostalgia, put on your rose-tinted glasses and have a look at your day to day now: what are the things you might miss? Try to make more effort to mindfully embrace and enjoy those moments. This stage of life may be hard graft, but in a decade you will look back and tilt your head nostalgically, however much you may roll your eyes at this thought now.

Those days when you're muttering 'FFS!' under your breath because your toddler won't go in the damn buggy but instead wants to totter next to you, holding your hand, forcing you to slow down. Think about looking back on those days. You may remember the physicality, the relentlessness of it. But you'll sigh fondly when you remember the tiny hand reaching for yours, the beautiful wide eyes that gazed on you with such unfettered adoration.

'My third child loved being carried everywhere. I knew it wouldn't last forever so enjoyed it (mostly!). In the blink of an eye she's just turned six and is now almost too heavy to carry as she's like a sack of spuds #missthosedays.'

Lorna, mum of three

The family pie

Family therapy uses the metaphor of a pie.

- Think about a good quality 'family pie', and all the ingredients it needs, e.g. care and kindness, boundaries and rules, love, fun, etc.
- Decide on the best proportions of these for the pie to turn out well.
- What seasoning would you imagine it to need to really taste good (and for children to turn into well-adjusted content adults)?
- Look at the ingredients you have in your family pie, and check the amounts of each. It might be that some are missing or that there is too much or too little of some in there. What might you need to adjust to get the recipe just right?

'We all have different experiences of parenthood. I often find it hard to assimilate an image in my head of life as a successful, happy, independent, joyful woman, with putting away the washing and the drudgery of cleaning up food from the floor that will be spilled again within an hour or two. But despite all of that, moments of bliss are there to be had and they make it all worthwhile. Iris running up shouting "Mummy" and giving me an enormous hug when I've been back. Joseph working out how to ride a bike and grinning his face off. I'm learning that the best thing of all is to go with the flow, while paddling in the direction that's right for us. Just as with birth, this is as much about letting go of control as it is discovering what is within our power to influence. I'm trying to lean into the difficult times rather than resist them, and be honest about how it's going.'

Zoe, mum of two

Remember you're never fully dressed without a smile – fool your own body into feeling more joyful by simply smiling, even if you really don't feel like it. *Especially if you really don't feel like it.* It works, believe me. You can't have it all and you don't need to be perfect. As long as you are doing your best, even just thinking about hoping to do your best, that's good enough. Children are a gift, not (just) another job. Enjoy them, and you'll enjoy yourself so much more.

Final word: letting go of perfect

Brené Brown's TED talk on 'The Power of Vulnerability' is essential viewing for any mum who is struggling with the fall-out of supermum syndrome – and 28 million people agree.

She talks about how our courage is borne out of *vulnerability*, not strength. It takes courage to be imperfect. Parenting is a 'shame' and 'judgement' minefield, because most of us are wading through uncertainty and self-doubt when it comes to raising our children.

In her words: 'Shame drives two primary tapes: not good enough, and who do you think you are? ... it's a very formidable emotion. Its survival is based on us not talking about it, so it's done everything it can do to make it unspeakable.' So, if we all collectively talk more about the things that we worry make us 'not good enough' as parents, and gradually break down the hold that the myth of Supermum has over us, we'll realise we are, in fact, all good enough.

> 'The greatest gift that I can give to you is to live and love with my whole heart and to dare greatly. I will not teach or love or show you anything perfectly, but I will let you see me, and I will always hold sacred the gift of seeing you. Truly, deeply, seeing you.'
>
> Excerpt from Brené Brown's 'Parenting Manifesto'

Resources

Books

Brown, Stuart, *Play: How It Shapes the Brain, Opens the Imagination and Invigorates the Soul*, 2010, J. P. Tarcher/Penguin Putnam.

Cannon, Emma, *The Baby-Making Bible*, 2010, Pan Macmillan.

Figes, Kate, *Life After Birth*, 2008, Virago Press.

Greenberger, Dennis, and Christine Padesky, *Mind over Mood: Change How You Feel by Changing the Way You Think*, 2015, Guildford Press.

Hargreave, Bridget, *Fine (Not Fine): Perspectives and Experiences of Postnatal Depression*, 2015, Free Association Books.

Hooper, Clemmie, *How to Grow a Baby and Push it Out*, 2017, Vermillion.

James, Oliver, *How Not to F*** Them Up*, 2010, Vermillion.

Linehan, Marsha M., *DBT Skills Training Manual*, 2015, Guildford Press.

Mayall Fine, Phanella, and Alice Olins, *Step Up: Confidence, Success and Your Stellar Career in 10 Minutes a Day*, 2016, Penguin.

Millar, Fiona, *The Secret World of the Working Mother: Juggling Work, Kids and Sanity*, 2009, Vermillion.

Munsch, Robert, *Love You Forever*, 1999, Turtleback Books.

Myles, Pamela, and Roz Shafran, *The CBT Handbook*, 2015, Robinson.

Napthali, Sarah, *Buddhism For Mothers*, 2003, Allen & Unwin.

Ou, Heng, *The First Forty Days*, 2016, Abram Books.

Powell, Trevor, *The Mental Health Handbook: A Cognitive Behavioural Approach*, 2009, Routledge.

Russell, Tamara, *Mindfulness in Motion*, 2015, Watkins Publishing.

Sandberg, Sheryl, *Lean In: Women, Work and the Will to Lead*, 2013, WH Allen.

Stadlen, Naomi, *What Mothers Do: Especially when it looks like nothing*, 2004, Piatkus.

Stallard, Paul, *Think Good, Feel Good: A Cognitive Behaviour Therapy Workbook for Children and Young People*, 2002, Wiley-Blackwell.

Sunderland, Margot, *Draw on Your Emotions*, 1997, Routledge.

Turner, Sarah, *The Unmumsy Mum*, 2016, Bantam.

Vanderkam, Laura, *I Know How She Does It: How Successful Women Make the Most of Their Time*, 2015, Penguin.

Waldman, Ayelet, *Bad Mother*, 2010, Anchor Books.

Winnicott, D. W., *The Child, the Family and the Outside World*, 1964, Penguin.

Winnicott, D. W., *Playing and Reality*, 2005, Routledge.

Online articles

Brown, Brené, 'Parenting Manifesto': brenebrown.com/wp-content/uploads/2013/09/DaringGreatly-ParentingManifesto-light–8x10.pdf

Cannon, Emma, 'TED talk: It's About Time We Valued Being Fertile', https://m.youtube.com/watch?v=cxoZ7RIt3tQ

www.channel4.com/news/the-loneliness-of-becoming-a-new-mum

www.dulwichcentre.com.au/saying-hullo-again-Epston.pdf

www.edge.org/conversation/sarah_jayne_blakemore-the-adolescent-brain

goop.com/postnatal-depletion-even-10-years-later

www.theguardian.com/commentisfree/2016/may/10/perfect-mother-good-parenting-child-behaviour

www.theguardian.com/lifeandstyle/2008/aug/07/women.workandcareers

www.theguardian.com/lifeandstyle/2014/may/25/postnatal-depression-mothers-risk-child-four-years

www.theguardian.com/lifeandstyle/2015/aug/15/avoid-the-competitive-parent-trap

www.theguardian.com/lifeandstyle/2016/sep/29/self-harm-ptsd-and-mental-illness-soaring-among-young-women-in-england-survey

www.theguardian.com/lifeandstyle/2017/jan/09/born-mother-pregnancy-idea-frightening

www.hse.gov.uk/Statistics/overall/hssh1516.pdf?pdf=hssh1516

www.huffingtonpost.co.uk/entry/depression-and-anxiety-levels-are-on-the-rise-in-uk_uk_57e4e292e4b0e81629a97a2f

www.netmums.com/child/were-still-a-nation-of-sleep-deprived-parents-new-survey-reveals

www.independent.ie/life/family/mothers-babies/keep-calm-its-only-a-baby-why-parenting-shouldnt-be-a-contest–30167494.html

Jones, Lucy, 'Longed-for Child': http://somesuchstories.co/story/longed-for-child (2017)

www.madeformums.com/school-and-family/feeling-the-pressure-to-be-a-supermum/19594.html

McFadden, Joan, 'The power of talking sideways to children': www.theguardian.com/lifeandstyle/2017/jan/14/children-parents-talk-opportunities-sideways-listening-chats

media.psychologytools.com/worksheets/english_us/modifying_rules_and_assumptions_en-us.pdf

www.mirror.co.uk/lifestyle/family/secrets-super-mums-revealed-how-7693441

www.newscientist.com/article/2116527-becoming-a-mother-may-change-the-brain-to-read-babys-mind

www.npr.org/sections/13.7/2016/06/06/480906083/think-mothering-young-kids-is-hard-get-ready-for-even-tougher-times

www.researchgate.net/publication/280060065_Traditional_Postpartum_Practices_Among_Malaysian_Mothers_A_Review

www.selfishmother.com/how-i-got-my-mojo-back

www.thesundaytimes.co.uk/sto/news/uk_news/Society/article1687843.ece

www.ted.com/talks/brene_brown_on_vulnerability

Websites

Anxiety

www.anxietyuk.org.uk

Attunement

www.incredibleyears.com/programs/parent/babies-curriculum

CBT

www.rcpsych.ac.uk/mentalhealthinformation/therapies/cognitive behaviouraltherapy.aspx

DBT

www.mind.org.uk/information-support/drugs-and-treatments/
dialectical-behaviour-therapy-dbt

Fitting work around family life

Womenlikeus.org.uk

Mental health information, advice, support

Fundamental Facts about Mental Health 2016
www.mentalhealth.org.uk/publications/fundamental-facts-about-
mental-health–2016

Mental Health Foundation
www.mentalhealth.org.uk

Mind, the mental health charity
*Provides support and information for those suffering from mental health
issues.*
www.mind.org.uk

Rethink Mental Illness
*Gives expert, accredited advice and information to everyone affected by
mental health problems.*
www.rethink.org

Young Minds
*Advice and information on mental health for young people and parents
and carers.*
www.youngminds.org.uk

Mindfulness

bemindful.co.uk

www.mindful.org/meditation/mindfulness-getting-started

Postnatal depression

www.nct.org.uk/parenting/postnatal-depression

www.nhs.uk/conditions/stress-anxiety-depression/pages/mindful
ness.aspx

www.rcpsych.ac.uk/healthadvice/problemsdisorders/postnatal
depression.aspx

Blogs on birth, motherhood and beyond

antoniagodber.com – Nurturing new families blogspot

www.beccyhands.co.uk – doula, massage therapist

thebirthhub.co.uk/closing-bones-workshop

www.birthingmamasblog.com

confessionsofanicumum.blogspot.co.uk

emmacannon.co.uk

heyisthatme.co.uk

www.hypnobirthingplace.co.uk

toomuchmotheringinformation.com

theunmumsymum.blogspot.co.uk

Apps

Quility App: mindfulness on the go

Thought Diary: helps to analyse and reframe negative thoughts while providing psychoeducation about cognitive distortions/automatic dysfunctional thoughts.